ACTIVITIES TO SHARPEN CREATIVE WRITING SKILLS

BY CINDY BARDEN

ILLUSTRATIONS BY CORBIN HILLAM

Teaching & Learning Company

1204 Buchanan St., P.O. Box 10
Carthage, IL 62321

This book belongs to

_____

This book was developed for the Teaching & Learning Company
by The Good Neighbor Press, Inc., Grand Junction, CO.

Cover illustration by Corbin Hillam

Teaching & Learning Company
1204 Buchanan St., P.O. Box 10
Carthage, IL 62321

TABLE OF CONTENTS

Dear Teacher,

Writing is a way to communicate facts and ideas, to express thoughts and feelings and to tell a story. By using the reproducible activities in this book, you can encourage students to develop and sharpen creative writing skills, to stretch their imaginations and acquire critical thinking skills through a variety of prose and poetry activities.

In *Love to Write!* you'll find activities that provide students with the opportunity to explore and write various types of fiction, nonfiction and poetry. You can supplement these activities with additional instruction on grammar, punctuation, capitalization and other essential writing skills. **Suggestions for extended activities for every student activity are included in the back of the book.**

Works of literature other than novels, short stories, poetry and drama are considered nonfiction. This includes newspaper and magazine articles, textbooks, biographies and autobiographies. In a broader sense, nonfiction writing also includes letters, school reports, advertising copy, essays, instructional manuals and other types of everyday writing.

The word *nonfiction* is often equated with the word *true*—as opposed to made up. In nonfiction, the word *true* may need to be qualified to "true as seen by a specific individual." Sometimes fiction and nonfiction overlap, as in historical fiction.

Poetry can be more difficult to define. Ask 100 poets and you'll probably get 100 different definitions. The *New Webster's Dictionary of the English Language* (Lexicon Publications, Inc., 1992) defines *poetry* as "a type of discourse which achieves its effects by rhythm, sound patterns and imagery . . . the poetic form evokes emotions or sensations, but it may also serve to convey loftiness of tone, or to lend force to ideas."

That definition itself is so lofty in tone that if you use this definition in your class, you'll probably turn everyone off on poetry. When you talk about poetry with your students, keep the discussion light and simple.

You could explain that poetry is a form of literature which expresses feelings, thoughts or ideas about something through the use of specific words arranged in a specific order.

To help your students learn to write well, they need to do six things:

Read	**Read**	**Read**
	and	
Practice	**Practice**	**Practice**

Who knows? You may be encouraging a future Ernest Hemingway, Anne McCaffrey, William Shakespeare, e.e. cummings, Emily Dickinson or Jean Auel in your classroom. Even if none of your students ever become famous authors, the creative writing skills students learn from you are a gift they will benefit from for the rest of their lives.

Sincerely,

Cindy

Cindy Barden

HOW TO USE THIS BOOK

You'll find useful suggestions for extended activities in the back of the book for each of the student activity sheets. Many topics lend themselves to open, lively discussions. Vocabulary words are listed following appropriate activities.

Provide books of prose and poetry in the classroom for students to read in their free time. Frequently visit the library as a class. Read your favorite prose and poetry to the class. Be sure to include both rhymed poems and free verse. Ask them to listen to the sounds of the words as you read. Encourage students to read their own work to the class, at school assemblies and during student programs.

Collect students' writings and make booklets of their best work. You can photocopy the students' work and publish individual booklets or a class anthology. Invite students who enjoy art to contribute illustrations. Students and parents will treasure this collection of student writing.

Encourage students to illustrate their work. Students who don't like to draw might find it easier to sketch fancy borders around their poems. Show students you are proud of their work by displaying their stories and poems on bulletin boards in the classroom and throughout the school.

Students who have difficulty writing may find it helpful to develop their stories orally at first. A teacher aide or parent volunteer could write or tape the story as the student tells it.

All of the activities in this book are suitable for assessment programs. Students may establish a "Love to Write" portfolio and contribute completed activities throughout the year. Be sure to date each piece of work so that you may see an accurate progression. At the end of the year, you and the students may select samples for evaluation.

Learning to write well is a valuable asset, both in school and on the job. Young writers need to learn and develop skills that apply to all types of writing: the use of correct grammar, punctuation and capitalization, the ability to write complete, clear sentences and paragraphs and the ability to think and write critically and creatively.

ALL ABOUT ME

Here's good advice about writing: Write about what you know best. What subject do you know more about than anyone else in the world? Yourself.

An **autobiography** is a story you write about yourself. You can describe your whole life or one event that happened to you. You can write about how you felt at a certain time.

> Was your last birthday terrific?
> Did you travel someplace special last summer?
> How are things going in school?
> What did you do last Saturday?

These could be topics for a story about yourself.

Prewrite: Jot down ideas about events in your life you could write about.

Write a paragraph describing an event in your life.

_____

_____

_____

_____

_____

_____

_____

_____

_____

_____

_____

_____

_____

_____

_____

Draw a picture of yourself or tape one of your school pictures to this page.

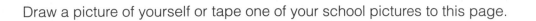

THIS IS YOUR LIFE

An **autobiography** can be about an event in your life. It can also be about how you felt about what happened.

> How did you feel when you moved to a new home?
> What happened that made you very happy, scared or proud?
> How do you feel when it storms?
> Have you ever felt embarrassed?

Your feelings are topics for a story about yourself.

Prewrite: Write a few words after each feeling to describe an event that made you feel this way.

Sad _____   Happy _____

Angry _____   Lonely _____

Scared _____   Jealous _____

Proud _____   Embarrassed _____

Frustrated _____   Joyful _____

Select one feeling to write about: _____

In one sentence, describe the event that made you feel that way.

_____

_____

Now write a short paragraph about how you felt.
Draw a picture of yourself when you felt that way.

_____

_____

_____

_____

_____

_____

_____

_____

_____

_____

This is me.

LONG, LONG AGO

How far back can you remember? Think back to kindergarten. Can you remember your first day of school? What about your fourth birthday? Can you think back even farther to when you were two or three years old?

Close your eyes. Relax. Let your mind wander backwards. What is your earliest memory?

Describe your earliest memory.

▓ DEAR JOURNAL

A journal or diary is a record you keep of your thoughts and ideas. In your journal, you don't have to worry about writing complete sentences or spelling every word correctly. Unless you wish to share what you write in your journal, no one else will read it.

People who keep journals usually write in them a little bit every day. Sometimes they draw pictures or write poems.

What could you write about in your journal?

- Your feelings about yourself
- Your feelings about other people
- Your hopes and dreams
- Ideas for stories or poems

List other ideas for topics you could write about in your journal.

Start a journal in a notebook. Write in it every day. Sometimes, go back and read what you wrote.

If you can't think of anything to write about one day, go back and look at your list of ideas.

▚ THE WHOLE STORY

To be complete, a story must have a beginning, a middle and an ending.

- ■ The beginning introduces the character and his or her problem.
- ■ The middle tells what the character does and what happens.
- ■ The ending tells how the character solves the problem and how the story ends.

Read a short story, then answer the questions below.

What is the name of the story? _____

Who is the main character? _____

What is the character's problem? _____

_____

How soon do you find out what the problem is? _____

_____

How are the character and the problem introduced? _____

_____

How does the character solve the problem? _____

_____

How does the story end? _____

_____

Summarize the story in one sentence. _____

_____

_____

Does the story have a good beginning? Why or why not? _____

_____

_____

Does the story have a good ending? Why or why not?

_____

_____

_____

_____

_____

_____

_____

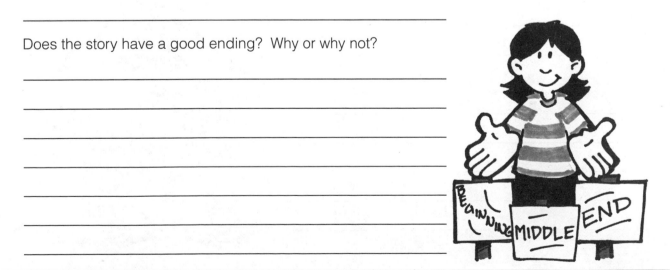

■ ONCE UPON A TIME

When a story begins, "Once upon a time . . ." you know it will be a made-up story, not a true story. Another beginning for a fiction story might be "In days of old, when dragons roamed the earth . . ."

Look through fiction stories. Write the first sentence from three stories below.

1. _____

   _____

   _____

2. _____

   _____

   _____

3. _____

   _____

   _____

Writers try to make the first sentence interesting so readers will want to keep reading. Did the writer do a good job on the beginning sentences you read?

Select one of the above sentences and think about how that sentence could be more interesting or exciting.

Rewrite one of the sentences.

_____

_____

_____

_____

_____

_____

_____

_____

_____

TLC10017 Copyright © Teaching & Learning Company, Carthage, IL 62321

▌TALE OF A PEACOCK

Select four numbers from 1 to 10. You may choose four different numbers or the same number more than once. Write your numbers here: ____ ____ ____ ____

Now look at the four sections below. The four numbers you selected will be the first sentence of your story.

If you selected 4, 2, 1 and 5, the first sentence of your story would be: A nimble mountain goat walked among the sharks under the picnic table.

Write the first sentence of your story on another sheet of paper. Then finish the story. Be creative, silly or serious. Don't forget to give your story a title.

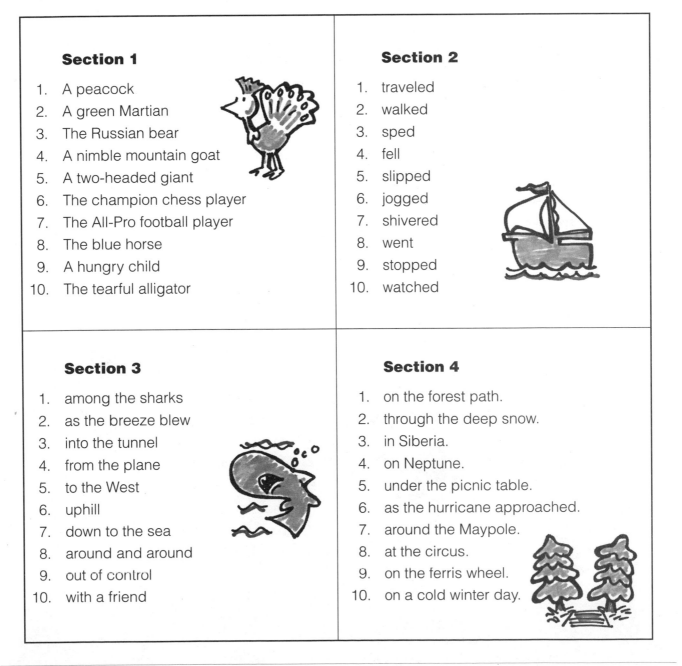

Section 1

1. A peacock
2. A green Martian
3. The Russian bear
4. A nimble mountain goat
5. A two-headed giant
6. The champion chess player
7. The All-Pro football player
8. The blue horse
9. A hungry child
10. The tearful alligator

Section 2

1. traveled
2. walked
3. sped
4. fell
5. slipped
6. jogged
7. shivered
8. went
9. stopped
10. watched

Section 3

1. among the sharks
2. as the breeze blew
3. into the tunnel
4. from the plane
5. to the West
6. uphill
7. down to the sea
8. around and around
9. out of control
10. with a friend

Section 4

1. on the forest path.
2. through the deep snow.
3. in Siberia.
4. on Neptune.
5. under the picnic table.
6. as the hurricane approached.
7. around the Maypole.
8. at the circus.
9. on the ferris wheel.
10. on a cold winter day.

A LARGE PURPLE DRAGON DID WHAT?

Select four numbers from 1 to 10. You may choose four different numbers or the same number more than once. Write your numbers here: _____   _____   _____   _____

Now look at the four sections below. The four numbers you selected will be the first sentence of your story.

If you chose 4, 9, 3 and 4, the first sentence of your story would be: A huge hairy spider cried in the desert on a red skateboard.

Write the first sentence of your story on another sheet of paper. Then finish the story. Be creative, silly or serious. Don't forget to give your story a title.

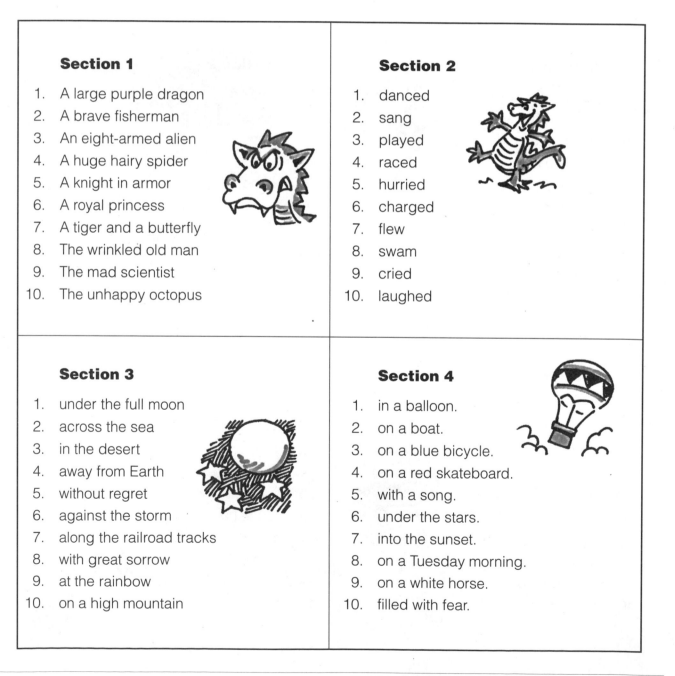

Section 1

1. A large purple dragon
2. A brave fisherman
3. An eight-armed alien
4. A huge hairy spider
5. A knight in armor
6. A royal princess
7. A tiger and a butterfly
8. The wrinkled old man
9. The mad scientist
10. The unhappy octopus

Section 2

1. danced
2. sang
3. played
4. raced
5. hurried
6. charged
7. flew
8. swam
9. cried
10. laughed

Section 3

1. under the full moon
2. across the sea
3. in the desert
4. away from Earth
5. without regret
6. against the storm
7. along the railroad tracks
8. with great sorrow
9. at the rainbow
10. on a high mountain

Section 4

1. in a balloon.
2. on a boat.
3. on a blue bicycle.
4. on a red skateboard.
5. with a song.
6. under the stars.
7. into the sunset.
8. on a Tuesday morning.
9. on a white horse.
10. filled with fear.

ONE, TWO, THREE, LET'S WRITE TOGETHER

Sometimes two or more writers work together on a story. You and two classmates can work together to write a story. Follow the directions below. Write as neatly as you can.

1. Student 1 writes two or three sentences to begin the story.

   _____

   _____

   _____

2. Student 2 writes two or three sentences to continue the story.

   _____

   _____

   _____

3. Student 3 writes two or three sentences to end the story.

   _____

   _____

   _____

4. One student can read the story out loud to the other two or to the class. Write the title for your story here.

   _____

Were you happy with how the story turned out?

Try this again with other classmates. Use the same beginning, but let two other people write the middle and ending.

How is the second story different? Which one do you like better?

DESIGNING A PLAN

When architects design houses, the first step is to draw a plan they will follow.

To write a story, writers often follow a plan. Like an architect, a writer may change the plan as often as necessary.

Let's plan a book for young children (kindergarten or first grade).

First: Write your plan by answering these questions:

Who or what is the main character? _____

What other characters will be in the story? _____

_____

Where does the story take place? _____

When does the story take place? _____

What problems do the main characters face? _____

_____

What action takes place? _____

_____

What exciting events happen? _____

_____

How is the problem solved? _____

_____

What happens in the end? _____

_____

What is the title? _____

Go back and read your plan. Go ahead and make changes if you want. Now write the first sentence of your story.

_____

_____

_____

_____

_____

_____

_____

◼ BUILDING A STORY

Use your story plan to write the first draft of a story. Remember, this is a story for young children. Keep the words simple and the sentences short.

Go back and read your story plan. Cross out words and make as many changes to the story plan as you want.

Write your story here.

_____ *(title)*

_____

_____

_____

_____

_____

_____

_____

_____

_____

_____

_____

_____

_____

_____

_____

_____

_____

_____

_____

Since this is a story for young children,
add an illustration to go with your story.

◧ THE REST OF THE STORY

The first sentence of a story can be the hardest to write. Select one of the beginnings listed below and write the rest of the story.

- Josh, a large purple gorilla, was hungry. He went looking for something to eat.

- Frank looked in his closet and couldn't believe what he saw.

- Sashiko hoped her teacher would understand why she didn't do her homework last night. She didn't do her homework because . . . .

- On their way home from school, Meagan and Carlo saw three men chasing a penguin down Park Avenue.

- Tasha felt lonely as she looked at the sunset.

- "Can I keep him, Mom?" Devan asked. He pointed to the _____ that had followed him home from the zoo.

- Mr. Crabtree spotted Jake and Ariel by his apple tree. He said, . . ."

Write the rest of your story here.

_____

_____

_____

_____

_____

_____

_____

_____

_____

_____

_____

_____

_____

■⬛ PART TWO

Sometimes stories end too soon. What happened to the main character after the story ended? Did she go on to play in the Major League? Did he ever find a way to solve his problem? Did the twins have other adventures?

Think of a story you've read. Write questions that were not answered at the end of the story.

_____

_____

_____

_____

_____

Sometimes authors write more books or stories about the same characters. These are called **sequels**.

Write a sequel to the story that answers at least two of the questions you listed.

_____

_____

_____

_____

_____

_____

_____

_____

WRITE FROM EXPERIENCE

Write what you know about. Write from your own experiences, but don't limit yourself. Use your past experiences to imagine new situations or places.

You could write about things that happened . . .

in school   at home   in your neighborhood   at a park   at the mall

What happened or might have happened that you could write about?

_____

_____

_____

You could write about people you know . . . **friends   family   neighbors   classmates**

Name several people you know or would like to meet (real or imaginary).

_____

_____

_____

You could write about things you've done . . .

ride a horse   fly in a plane   walk in the woods

What have you done or would like to do that you could write about?

_____

_____

_____

You could write about places you've been . . . **on vacation   a zoo   the circus**

What places could you write about that you've seen or would like to visit?

_____

_____

_____

What are some things in your life you'd like to change?

_____

_____

_____

Select one of these topics and write a paragraph or short story on another sheet of paper.

GET TO KNOW SOMEONE

A true story written about someone is called a biography. To write a biography, you need to get to know the person. You can do that by asking questions in an interview.

Who would you like to write about?_____

Prepare questions to ask before you do an interview. Questions you could ask are:

- When and where were you born?
- When did you move to this neighborhood?
- What type of work do you do?
- What kind of music do you like?
- What is the most exciting thing that ever happened to you?

Finish writing these questions.

What is your favorite _____?

How do you feel about _____?

Would you like to visit _____?

When did you _____?

How do you_____?

Why do you_____?

Where did you learn _____?

What is your best _____?

Write at least three more questions you could ask in an interview.

_____

_____

_____

Set up a time to do your interview. Take your list of questions, a pencil or pen and plenty of writing paper. If you think of other questions not on your list, go ahead and ask.

THE LIFE AND TIMES OF SOMEONE SPECIAL

A biography is a true story about someone. You did an interview to learn more about someone. Now you are ready to begin writing a biography.

Read the answers you wrote during your interview. What part of the person's life do you want to write about?

Prewrite: Write words to describe the person you interviewed. How does he look? What is she like? What features or qualities are the most outstanding?

_____

_____

_____

Copy words and phrases from your notes that you might use to write the biography.

_____

_____

_____

What will you title this biography? _____

Draw a sketch of the person on the cover of the book below.

Write the first draft of the biography on the back of this page. Look back at your notes as you write. If you think of questions you forgot to ask, write them down. Contact the person for answers.

Make corrections and changes to your first draft. Write the final biography on another sheet of paper.

TITLES: AN INVITATION TO READ

What makes you decide to read a book or story? Did a friend tell you it was a funny story? Was the picture on the cover interesting?

What about the title? Titles often tell us something about the story like *Alexander and the Terrible, Horrible, No Good, Very Bad Day* or *Tales of a Fourth Grade Nothing*. Some titles use the name of the main character: *The Adventures of Tom Sawyer*, *Black Beauty* and *David Copperfield*.

Look at the titles of books and stories in your classroom or library. Write three titles that tell something about the story and three titles that use the name of a main character.

Titles That Tell About the Story	**Titles That Name a Main Character**
_____	_____
_____	_____
_____	_____

Write titles of your own for these stories.

A mystery story about a lost key

_____

A story about a princess and storm

_____

A story about Jilha and a trip to Mars

_____

A funny story about a squirrel

_____

A scary story about something under the bed

_____

Make up two titles. Write one sentence about the story.

Title: _____

This story is about _____

_____

Title: _____

This story is about _____

_____

JEB HOPPED, SKIPPED AND JUMPED

Verbs are words that show action or being. *Climb, dance, run, sit, sleep* are action verbs. *Was, is, am* and *are* are also verbs.

Action verbs make your writing more interesting.

Write ten different verbs to finish these sentences:

John _____ to the mall.   Marla _____ all day.

1. _____   1. _____
2. _____   2. _____
3. _____   3. _____
4. _____   4. _____
5. _____   5. _____
6. _____   6. _____
7. _____   7. _____
8. _____   8. _____
9. _____   9. _____
10. _____   10. _____

Cut out a picture from a newspaper or magazine and tape or glue it to the back of this page. Write as many verbs as you can to describe the action in the picture.

TLC10017 Copyright © Teaching & Learning Company, Carthage, IL 62321

STUDENT WRITES AWARD-WINNING HEADLINES

A headline in a newspaper or magazine tells you what the story will be about. Headlines are usually short—no more than five or six words. Words like *a, an* and *the* usually do not appear in headlines.

Look through newspapers or magazines. Cut out three headlines and glue or tape them to the back of this page.

How many words are there in each headline you selected?

_____   _____   _____

Run, discovers, moves, won, escapes, crashes are action verbs.

What action verbs are used in the headlines you selected?

_____   _____   _____

Write other action verbs that could be used in headlines.

_____

_____

_____

How are headlines like titles of books and stories?

_____

_____

_____

How are headlines different than titles of books and stories?

_____

_____

_____

■ ASTRONAUTS DISCOVER LIFE ON MARS!
MAIL DELIVERED 50 YEARS LATE!
VOLCANO ERUPTS IN JAPAN!

Headlines use strong action words. Write three headlines about something that happened to you. Use strong action words. Do not use i*s, was* or *to be.*

Some headlines use **alliteration**—several words that begin with the same letter or sound.

PETER PIPER PICKED A PECK OF PETUNIAS
SPARROWS SAVE SEATTLE

Finish these headlines using alliteration and strong action verbs.

TOURIST TRAVELS TO _____

CLEVELAND CELEBRATES _____

TORNADO TERRORIZES _____

FOOTBALL FANS _____

RAIN RUINS _____

FRED _____

MAYOR _____

WHALE WATCHERS _____

Use alliteration to write a headline about yourself.

_____

ANSWER THE SIX QUESTIONS

The first one or two sentences of a newspaper article should give the reader enough information to answer six important questions:

Who?   **What?**   **When?**   **Where?**   **Why?**   **How?**

The foreman of a construction crew in Topeka, Kansas, called scientists to the
building site of a new hotel yesterday after workers discovered
dinosaur bones while digging the foundation.

Who?   The foreman of a construction crew

What?   Called scientists

When?   Yesterday

Where?   In Topeka, Kansas

Why?   Because workers discovered dinosaur bones

How?   By digging a foundation for a new hotel

Write a headline for the above article. _____

A stranger helped Mrs. Jackson find her glasses after she slipped on a banana
peeling and fell in front of Groucho's Grocery last Tuesday. He said Mrs.
Jackson reminded him of his grandmother.

Answer the six questions using information in the above sentences.

Who?   _____

What?   _____

When?   _____

Where?   _____

Why?   _____

How?   _____

Write a headline for the above article. _____

Write one or two sentences to start an article about something that happened to you recently.
Be sure to answer the six questions.

_____

_____

_____

_____

Write a headline for your article. _____

▚ TOOLS OF THE TRADE

What do you need to be a writer? A pen or pencil and a piece of paper? A computer? A desk? All of these items are useful.   A **dictionary** and a **thesaurus** are other valuable tools.

A dictionary helps you find the meanings and correct spellings of words. It tells you how to pronounce them.

A thesaurus is like a dictionary but different. Instead of giving you the meanings of words, it gives you a list of similar words.

Look up the word *walk* in the dictionary. Write one definition of *walk*.

_____

_____

Now look up *walk* in a thesaurus. Write six words listed under *walk* in the thesaurus.

_____

_____

Compare the dictionary definition and the thesaurus listings for other words. How are they different?

Dictionary _____

_____

Thesaurus _____

_____

Dictionary _____

_____

Thesaurus _____

_____

Name _____

IN OTHER WORDS

A synonym is a word with the same or similar meaning as another word. Authors often use synonyms to make their writing more interesting.

- The <u>big</u> dog ran up the <u>big</u> hill. ■ His <u>big</u> tail wagged happily.

Instead of using the word *big* three times, an author could write:

- The <u>huge</u> dog ran up the <u>steep</u> hill. ■ His <u>long</u> tail wagged happily.

Substitute words with the same or similar meanings for the ones underlined in the sentences below.

The <u>happy</u> clown smiled when he made the children <u>happy</u>.

_____   _____

The <u>tired</u> woman put her <u>tired</u> feet on the stool.

_____   _____

A **thesaurus** can give you many synonyms for a word. Remember, a synonym may not always have *exactly* the same meaning. If you use a thesaurus, make sure you know the meaning of the word before you use it as a substitute. It may not be the right word.

Look up these words in a thesaurus. Write several synonyms for each word.

sad _____

good _____

nice _____

thing _____

person _____

pretty _____

rain _____

object _____

went _____

contest _____

party _____

walk _____

bright _____

dark _____

said _____

loud _____

█ UP, DOWN, OVER, UNDER

Antonyms are words that mean the opposite. Up—down, in—out, boy—girl are antonyms. A thesaurus usually gives antonyms for words. Some dictionaries also list antonyms.

Write antonyms for these words. Use a dictionary or thesaurus if you need help finding an antonym.

big _____	right _____
east _____	eat _____
sleep _____	run _____
tall _____	quiet _____
happy _____	child _____
efficient _____	fix _____
solo _____	cheerful _____
smile _____	expensive _____
baby _____	near _____
round _____	flat _____
long _____	dark _____
mountain _____	sit _____
succeed _____	work _____

How many antonyms can you find in this picture?

◼▦ LOOK IT UP

Writers use many types of **reference** books to find information.

◾ If you wanted to write a report or story about a penguin, how would you find out how long it takes for a penguin egg to hatch?

◾ If you were writing about a trip from Chicago to Dublin, Ireland, how would you find out how far apart the two cities are?

◾ If you wanted to describe a girl in India, how would you know what clothes she would wear?

What kind of books would you look in to find the answers to the questions below? You can list more than one type of reference.

How far is it from Moscow to London?

_____

When it is noon in California, what time is it in New York?

_____

What is the second verse of your country's national anthem?

_____

Who was the third President of the United States?

_____

What were John F. Kennedy's wife and children's names?

_____

Who wrote *The Lion, the Witch and the Wardrobe*?

_____

What was the name of the pig in *Charlotte's Web*?

_____

What day of the week will Christmas be on this year?

_____

Who starred in the movie *Old Yeller*?

_____

What is the capital of China?

_____

How many people live in New York City?

_____

▚ GREAT IDEA!

Another "tool of the trade" for writers is a good imagination. Ideas for stories and poems can be found all around you. All you have to do is look and listen.

Name places you can find ideas.

_____

_____

_____

_____

When you think of a good idea for a story, write it down and keep it until you're ready to work on it. Many writers keep an "idea notebook" or "idea folder." Some writers keep their ideas in a shoe box.

What's wrong with simply keeping your ideas in your head?

_____

_____

_____

_____

Where can you keep your ideas?

_____

_____

_____

Write three ideas for stories that you might use sometime.

_____

_____

_____

YOU CAN FIND IDEAS EVERYWHERE

DON'T LET GOOD IDEAS GET AWAY

When you have an idea for a story or a poem, write it down on this page. Keep this page in a notebook or folder where it won't get lost. Look back at your ideas when you need an idea for something to write about. Add new ideas as you think of them.

▚ WHAT IF?

Where do writers get ideas for stories? Ideas come from many sources—from a writer's imagination, experience and from watching people. Writers also get ideas by asking themselves "what if?"

"What if" questions can be the beginning of a great story. Did you ever wonder . . .

- What if you won a lottery?
- What if trees were purple?
- What if houses could talk?
- What if baseball was illegal?
- What if it rained dollar bills?
- What if zebras didn't have stripes?
- What if liver tasted like chocolate?
- What if people had wheels instead of feet?

Write your own "what if" questions. Be as silly or outrageous as you like.

What if _____?

What if _____?

What if _____?

What if _____?

To write a story, answer a "what if" question any way you want. There are no wrong answers.

Select one of the "what if" questions. Prewrite by jotting down ideas for an answer.

Use your ideas to write an answer to your "what if" question.

Write your final copy on another sheet of paper.

WHY WRITE LETTERS?

It's fun to receive letters in the mail. Usually, you have to write a letter to get one back.

Letters are divided into two types. **Friendly** letters are written to people you know personally. They are usually very informal. When you write a letter to friends, it's a lot like talking to them. **Business** letters are written to people you don't know or to companies. They are usually more formal.

Why write letters?

- A letter costs less than a long distance telephone call.
- You can plan your letter ahead of time.
- Letters can be read over and over.
- Request information about a place you'd like to visit.
- Compliment someone for a job well done.
- Complain about a product.

What other reasons can you think of to write letters?

_____

_____

Who could you write to?

- School friends who moved away
- Relatives who live far away
- A teacher who retired
- Pen pals around the world
- Newspapers
- Companies
- Politicians

Who else could you write to?

_____

_____

What could you write about? You could . . .

- write about your friends and family
- tell what's happening in school
- write about pets or hobbies
- ask questions

What else could you write about?

_____

_____

▐ WRITING A FRIENDLY LETTER

Use this format to write a friendly letter to someone you know.

Your name
Your street address
Your city, state, zip code

Name of the person you
are writing to, followed
by a comma

Dear _____,

Body of the letter: Use this space to write the rough draft of your letter.

_____

_____

_____

_____

_____

_____

_____

_____

_____

_____

Closing: Love,

                                                                        Your name

Rewrite your
letter on another
sheet of paper
and mail it.

Here's how to
address an
envelope.

Your name
Your street address
Your city, state, zip code

Place
stamp
here.

Name
Street address
City, state, zip code

WRITING A BUSINESS LETTER

You can write business letters for many reasons:

- ■ To find out about a place you'd like to visit
- ■ To ask an expert for information
- ■ To express your opinion to a newspaper or politician
- ■ To compliment an author on a book
- ■ To explain a problem with a product or service
- ■ To thank a restaurant or business for good service

What are other reasons to write a business letter?

Use this format to write a business letter.

Your name
Your street address
Your city, state, zip code

Name of person
Name of company
Street address
City, state, zip code

Name of the person you
are writing to, followed
by a colon

Dear _____: (Use Mr., Ms., Senator or other title of respect.)

Body of the letter: Use this space to write the rough draft of your letter.

_____

_____

_____

_____

_____

_____

Closing: Yours truly,

                                               Your name

■ SPEAK UP

Newspapers and magazines often publish letters from readers expressing their opinions. They may also print editorials—statements of opinion by the publication itself.

An editorial may contain a combination of facts and opinions. Read these sentences. Put an **O** in the blank if it is an opinion. Put an **F** in the blank if it is a fact.

_____ Seattle is the capital of Washington.

_____ Seattle is the best city in Washington.

_____ Many types of apples grow in Washington.

_____ The best apples grow in Washington.

_____ Brown shoes are more comfortable than black ones.

_____ Apple pie tastes better than spinach.

People write editorials for many reasons . . .

■ They might be upset about something, or
■ They want to thank people for voting for them, or
■ They hope to change the way other people think, or
■ They see a problem and want to suggest a solution or
■ They want others to join them in a cause.

People write editorials because they feel strongly about something and want others to know about their feelings.

What topics could kids write editorials about?

_____

_____

_____

■ SOUND OFF

Read this list of topics.

- ■ Wearing uniforms to school
- ■ Gangs in your neighborhood
- ■ Writing book reports
- ■ Attending school six days a week
- ■ Writing editorials
- ■ Giving speeches in class
- ■ Poetry
- ■ Your parents
- ■ A situation at a neighborhood playground
- ■ Traffic in your neighborhood
- ■ Visiting relatives
- ■ Moving Christmas to July
- ■ The best person to be class president
- ■ Your brother or sister
- ■ Being an only child
- ■ Living in a single-parent family
- ■ Getting up early every morning

Select one topic you feel strongly about. Write an editorial to express your opinion.

To the Editor:

_____

_____

_____

_____

_____

_____

_____

_____

_____

_____

_____

_____

▞ STOP, LOOK, LISTEN

- Look around you. What do you see?
- Now close your eyes. What do you hear?
- Take a deep breath. What do you smell?

Take time to look, listen and smell all the details around you.

Use words and phrases to describe what you see, hear and smell.

What I see: _____

_____

_____

_____

_____

What I hear: _____

_____

_____

_____

What I smell: _____

_____

_____

_____

_____

SEE   HEAR   SMELL

PICTURE THIS

Josh, Maria and Alex were in the park flying Maria's new box kite. Suddenly, the wind blew the kite into an apple tree. Write a story about what the children do.

_____ (title)

_____

_____

_____

_____

_____

_____

_____

_____

_____

_____

_____

_____

_____

When you finish, add a title to your story on the line under the picture.

WELCOME TO DUNCAN'S CAVE

Duncan lives in this cave. Write a short story to answer these questions:

- Who or what is Duncan?
- Why does Duncan live in a cave?
- What does Duncan do in the cave?
- Describe the smells, sounds and sights of Duncan's cave.

_____
_____
_____
_____
_____
_____
_____
_____
_____
_____
_____
_____
_____
_____
_____
_____

GET INTO THE SCENE

Cut out a picture from a magazine that shows scenery. It could be a picture of mountains, water, the city, the country or any other place. Tape the picture to the back of this page. Study it carefully. Imagine you are present in the scene.

- What do you see?
- What do you hear?
- What do you smell?
- Do you taste anything?
- Who is with you?
- What are you thinking about?

Describe yourself in this scene.

_____

_____

_____

_____

_____

_____

_____

_____

SHARON'S MAGIC HAT

Sharon has a magic hat. When she puts it on, something very strange and wonderful happens.

Draw Sharon's hat. Write a story about what happens when Sharon puts on her wonderful hat.

_____

_____

_____

_____

_____

_____

_____

_____

_____

_____

_____

_____

_____

_____

_____

_____

■ AND THEN WHAT HAPPENED?

What will happen next? Draw a picture to show what you think will happen next. Write an ending to go with your drawing.

WHAT'S BEHIND THE DOOR?

A surprise waits behind this door. Is it a good surprise or a scary one? What do you think it will be? The only way to find out is to open it.

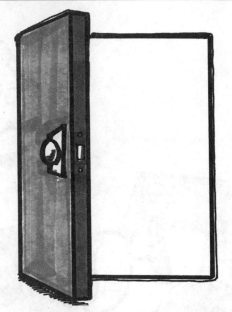

Finish the picture to show what's behind the door. How did you feel when you saw what was behind the door? Write a short story about what happened when you opened the door.

_____

_____

_____

_____

_____

_____

_____

_____

_____

_____

_____

_____

_____

_____

_____

▓ WHAT AM I?

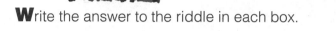

Write the answer to the riddle in each box.

I swim in the ocean, but I am not a fish.

I eat tiny plants and animals.

I'm larger than an elephant.

What am I?_____

I'm shaped something like an egg.

I'm covered with leather.

People kick me around.

What am I?_____

Write a riddle to describe one of these objects:

a cave	**a computer**	**an envelope**	**a book**
a mirror	**a ladder**	**the U.S. flag**	**a rope**

_____

_____

_____

What am I?

Think of another animal or object you could describe. Write a riddle about it.

_____

_____

_____

What am I?

Read your riddle to the class. Can your classmates solve it?

◼️ TELL ME ABOUT IT

How could you describe an object to someone who has never seen anything like it? You could describe its color, size and shape. You could describe what it's made of and what it's used for. You could describe what it smells like or what sounds it makes.

How would you describe these objects to someone from another planet who has never seen one before?

an egg	**a checkerboard**	**a cereal bowl**	**a TV**
a book	**a shoe**	**a telephone**	**a rug**
a fan	**a bed**	**a picnic table**	**scissors**

Prewrite: Select one of the objects. Write words and phrases to describe it.

_____

_____

_____

_____

Write a paragraph describing this object. Be very clear and very specific. Remember, you are talking to someone from another planet who has never seen one before.

_____

_____

_____

_____

_____

_____

_____

_____

_____

_____

_____

_____

_____

Name _____

▮▮ FEEL IT

Your sense of touch tells you sandpaper is rough and silk is smooth. Use words or short phrases to describe how these objects feel when you touch them.

velvet:_____

corduroy: _____

a pine tree: _____

sand: _____

water: _____

honey: _____

oil:_____

rope:_____

soap: _____

a man's face when he needs a shave:_____

Your sense of touch isn't limited to your hands. Use words or short phrases to describe how these things feel.

Mud squishing through your toes: _____

A breeze on a warm day: _____

Walking barefoot on wet grass:_____

Walking barefoot on hot concrete: _____

The wind in your hair as you ride a bike down a steep hill: _____

Dangling your feet in cool water on a hot day:_____

How your stomach feels as you ride a roller coaster: _____

A yawn: _____

The feel of ice cream in your mouth: _____

How your head feels when you have a cold: _____

What else can you feel with other parts of your body? List some examples.

_____

_____

_____

TLC10017 Copyright © Teaching & Learning Company, Carthage, IL 62321 〰 43

TWO SCENTS WORTH

Imagine the smell of fresh chocolate chip cookies. What a delicious, chocolaty smell! Adding details about what a character smells can make a story more interesting.

Read these phrases. Describe the smells.

hot cinnamon rolls: _____

fresh baked bread: _____

popcorn: _____

a wet dog: _____

hay: _____

pizza: _____

garlic: _____

a skunk: _____

a rose: _____

a barn: _____

fresh hot tar: _____

a turkey roasting: _____

gym socks: _____

Smells are often related to memories. Do any of the above smells bring back a memory? Write about a memory connected with a smell.

_____

_____

_____

_____

_____

_____

_____

_____

_____

_____

_____

GIVE ME AN EXAMPLE, PLEASE

When you **define** a word, you explain what it means. The word *swan* could be defined as a large bird with white feathers. Dictionaries give definitions of words.

Define these words. Use a dictionary if you get stuck.

table: _____

desk: _____

TV: _____

cinnamon: _____

elephant: _____

spring: _____

mystery: _____

door: _____

telephone: _____

Another way to define something is to give an example of something similar and tell how it is different. A swan is like a goose, but it has white feathers. Giving examples helps clarify what you mean when you write.

Define these words by giving examples.

An antelope is like _____

_____

A gate is like _____

_____

A buffalo is like _____

_____

A videotape is like _____

_____

A computer is like_____

_____

A crayon is like _____

_____

A pickup truck is like _____

_____

ROCK AND ROLL

Gather several small rocks of any shape and color, the more unusual the better. Line the rocks up in front of you and stare at them for ten minutes. Turn them over. Look at them from different angles.

What do the shapes make you think of? Do any of them look like people's heads? Draw faces on them with markers if you'd like.

Draw your rocks in the box below.

Write a story about one or more of the rocks you collected or about something one of the rocks reminds you of. Be creative or silly.

◼ HOW ARE THEY ALIKE?

To **compare** objects or ideas means to look for ways they are alike.

Select two objects from this list. Circle them. List five or more ways they are alike.

elephant   peanut   cactus   whale   tree   puppy   lawn   acorn

_____

_____

_____

_____

_____

_____

Select two objects from this second list. Circle them. List five or more ways they are alike.

computer   bridge   mountain   ocean   toothbrush   camera
pencil   shoe   clothespin   cloud   shaving cream   mouse

_____

_____

_____

_____

_____

_____

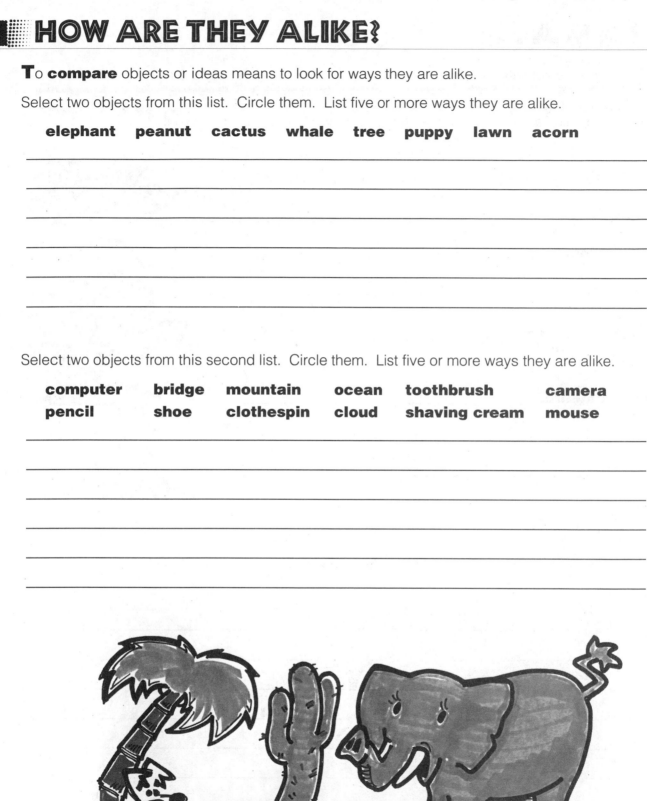

I AM A...

To **compare** objects, people or ideas means to look for ways they are alike.

What animal could you compare yourself to? Do you like to sleep during the day and stay up late at night like an owl? Are you as timid as a rabbit or as fast as a gazelle?

Write a few words to compare yourself to the animals listed.

dog: _____

porcupine: _____

deer: _____

fox: _____

bear: _____

hummingbird: _____

frog: _____

shark: _____

ostrich: _____

Write a paragraph comparing yourself to an animal.

I am like a _____ because _____

_____

_____

_____

_____

_____

_____

_____

_____

_____

_____

HOW ARE THEY DIFFERENT?

To **contrast** objects, ideas or people means to look at ways they are different.

Select two objects from this list. Circle them. List five or more ways they are different.

top hat	**sombrero**	**Stetson**
stocking cap	**baseball cap**	**football helmet**
derby	**beret**	**straw hat**

_____

_____

_____

_____

_____

_____

_____

Select two objects from the second list. Circle them. List five or more ways they are different.

spider	**butterfly**	**mosquito**	**fly**	**ant**
moth	**caterpillar**	**dragonfly**	**scorpion**	**bee**

_____

_____

_____

_____

_____

_____

A LOT LIKE ME

Do fictional characters ever remind you of yourself? Do they look, talk, think, feel or face problems like you? Do some fictional characters look and act very differently than you?

To **compare** means "to look for similarities." To **contrast** means "to look for differences."

Compare and contrast yourself to a fictional character. Name a character from a book, story or comic strip.

_____

List ways you are like that character.

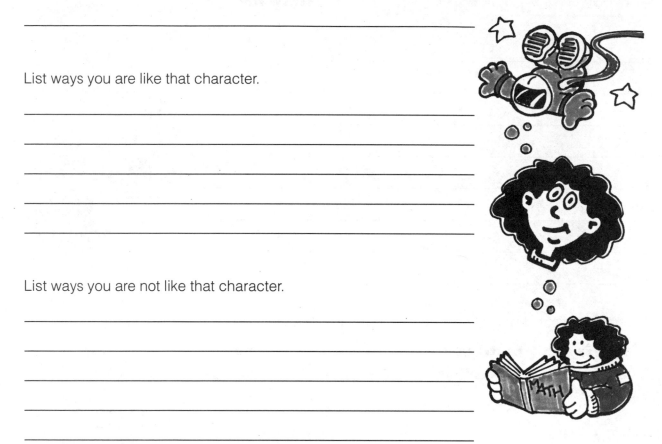

_____
_____
_____
_____

List ways you are not like that character.

_____
_____
_____
_____

Use the ideas you listed to compare and contrast yourself to the fictional character.

_____
_____
_____
_____
_____
_____
_____
_____

▦ IM-POSSIBLES

Impossible situations can make great ideas for stories.

- ■ I got sunburned last night at the beach.
- ■ I flew through the water.
- ■ I drank a hamburger for supper.
- ■ I built a snowman last July.
- ■ I swam across the Rocky Mountains.
- ■ As I looked in the mirror, I saw my hair turn green.
- ■ The mouse was larger than an elephant.
- ■ I stepped through the door and came out on Venus.

Think of several impossible situations. Write them here.

_____

_____

_____

_____

Use one of the "couldn't be's" listed above or one you made up as the basis for a short story.

_____

_____

_____

_____

_____

_____

_____

_____

_____

_____

_____

_____

_____

_____

◼ A DIFFERENT WAY TO LOOK AT THE WORLD

What if you were 20 feet (6 m) tall? What would a spoon be good for? What if you were only 2 inches (5.08 cm) tall? How would the spoon be useful?

Think about how different objects would look and how they could be used if a person were much larger or much smaller than usual. For each object listed below, write two uses for someone 20 feet (6 m) tall and someone 2 inches (5.08 cm) tall.

20 feet (6 m) tall　　　　　　　　　　**2 inches (5.08 cm) tall**

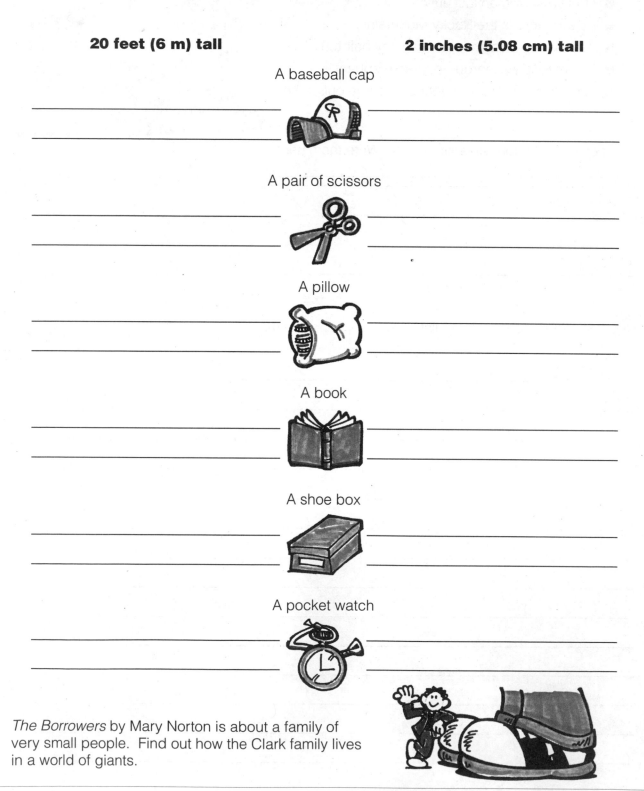

A baseball cap

_____　　　_____

_____　　　_____

A pair of scissors

_____　　　_____

_____　　　_____

A pillow

_____　　　_____

_____　　　_____

A book

_____　　　_____

_____　　　_____

A shoe box

_____　　　_____

_____　　　_____

A pocket watch

_____　　　_____

_____　　　_____

The Borrowers by Mary Norton is about a family of very small people. Find out how the Clark family lives in a world of giants.

AS TALL AS A TREE, AS SMALL AS A BEE

When Alice followed the white rabbit into the hole, she had many curious adventures and met many strange characters. When she ate and drank, she grew taller or smaller.

Prewrite. Use words and phrases to answer the questions.

What if you were ten times taller and everything else in the world stayed the same? What problems would you have?

_____

_____

What advantages would you have?

_____

_____

Would you like to be 50 feet (15 m) tall? Why or why not?

_____

_____

What if you were ten times smaller and everything else in the world stayed the same? What problems would you have?

_____

What advantages would you have?

_____

_____

Would you like to be 5 inches (12.7 cm) tall? Why or why not?

_____

_____

_____

On another sheet of paper, write a short story about someone who is 50 feet (15 m) tall or only 5 inches (12.7 cm) tall. Use words and phrases from the prewriting section above.

Have you seen the movie *Honey, I Shrunk the Kids*?

◼ THREE WISHES

Wouldn't it be great to have three wishes or a magic genie that appears when you rub a lamp? Would you use your wishes wisely?

If you could have three wishes, what would they be?

1. _____
   _____

2. _____
   _____

3. _____
   _____

If one of your wishes were granted, how would it change your life?

Write a short story about what would happen if you were granted one of your wishes.

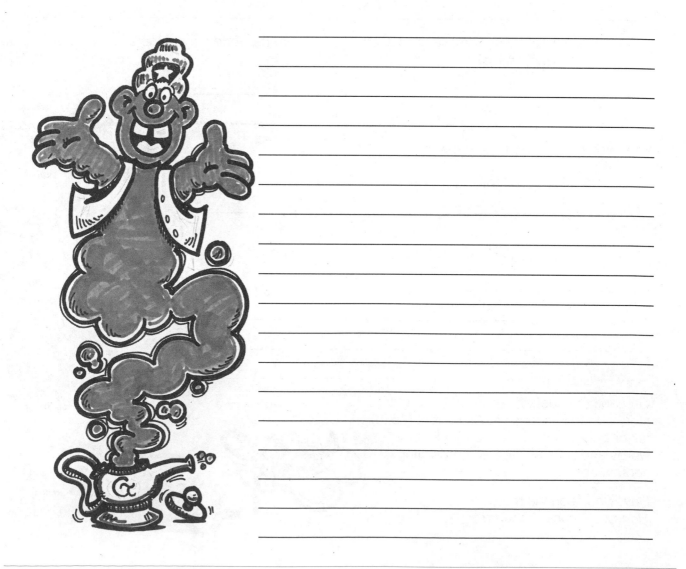

BEYOND SPACE AND TIME

Science fiction and fantasy stories can take place on other planets, real or imaginary. Sometimes they take place in other realities. For example, what would our country be like if England had won the Revolutionary War?

The setting may be in the past, present or future. People may have developed strange mental powers or invented wonderful new machines. Animals that talk or strange alien beings may live in fantasy worlds. Anything is possible.

Set the scene for a science fiction or fantasy story of your own.

Where does your story take place?_____

Describe the place. _____

_____

When does your story take place? _____

What is different about that time and place?_____

_____

_____

What types of people, aliens or animals will be in your story?_____

_____

_____

Describe the main character._____

_____

What problem does the main character have?_____

_____

What are some possible solutions to the character's problem?_____

_____

_____

What might happen in your story?_____

_____

How might the story end?_____

_____

Use your ideas to write a science fiction or fantasy story on another sheet of paper. Illustrate one scene from your story.

▪ REDESIGN A CAR

Have you ever wondered why most cars look pretty much the same? Why couldn't a car be two stories tall like a double-decker bus? Why do cars have four wheels? Why not three or six wheels?

Couldn't cars have special equipment, like a periscope to see around corners?

Here's your chance to design something different. What changes would you make if you could redesign a car?

Draw your new, improved version below.

Explain the changes you made and why you made them.

_____

_____

_____

_____

_____

_____

▦ A GAME FOR TWO

You and a friend are riding in the back seat of the car. You're tired of looking at the scenery, but it will be another two hours before you get to the campground.

Make up a new game you and your friend can play to pass the time. You have the following items with you:

- ■ a notebook and a pencil
- ■ a deck of cards, missing two tens
- ■ 12 pennies
- ■ 3 dice

What is the name of your game?

_____

How do you play your game?

_____

_____

_____

_____

_____

_____

_____

_____

_____

_____

_____

_____

_____

_____

_____

ONE BY ONE

1. There are five objects in this picture: a child, kite, dog, sun and lake. In the following boxes, replace each of these objects, one at a time.

2. The kite is missing. Draw something to replace the kite. It could be something the child is holding, like a balloon or something anywhere else in the picture, like a cloud or a pumpkin.

3. The puppy is missing from this picture. Draw the new object you drew in the last box and something to replace the puppy.

4. Now draw your two objects and something to replace the lake.

5. This time draw your three objects, plus a new one to replace the sun.

Name _____

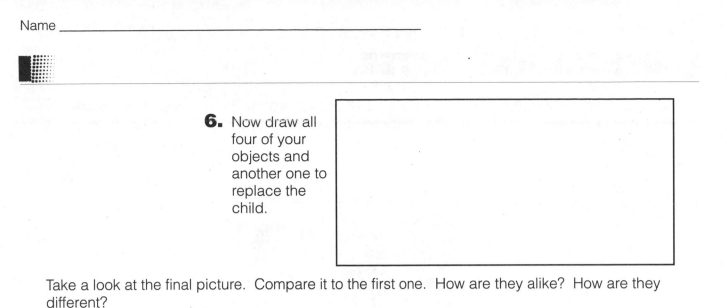

6. Now draw all four of your objects and another one to replace the child.

Take a look at the final picture. Compare it to the first one. How are they alike? How are they different?

Write a short story about what happens in the six boxes. Number each part of your story to match the correct box. You could start your story like this:

1. Last Saturday, Megan went to Silver Lake with her dog, Petunia. She flew her blue kite with the long red tail while Petunia chased a butterfly.

Name: _____

If you want to start the story another way, write your first sentence here.

_____

2. Suddenly, a big gust of wind blew the kite away. So Megan . . .

   _____

3. _____

   _____

4. _____

   _____

5. _____

   _____

6. _____

   _____

BEFORE AND AFTER

Look at the pictures below. Write one sentence that tells what might have happened before the event in the picture and what might happen after.

Before   **After**

_____

_____

_____

_____

_____

_____

_____

_____

_____

_____

_____

_____

_____

_____

_____

WHAT WAS THE QUESTION?

When someone else talks on the telephone, you hear one side of the conversation. In this case, you hear the answers but not the questions. Fill in a question for each answer listed below.

_____?

Fine, thank you.

_____?

Tomorrow, if the weather is good.

_____?

Probably not.

_____?

Sure, I can bring it to you.

_____?

I don't know.

_____?

That depends on Marla.

_____?

I don't remember.

_____?

They played well, but they lost.

_____?

I think it was blue.

PUT THE THINGAMABOB ON THE WHATCHACALLIT

Have you ever tried to follow directions to assemble something? Were the directions clear or confusing? Clear directions can make a difficult task simple to do. Confusing directions can make a simple task impossible.

To write clear directions, you need to break a task down into steps. Be sure to list the steps in order. What should you do first? What should you do next? Then what?

Think about how to do these tasks.

- Tie a shoe
- Replace a broken shoestring
- Prepare a bowl of cold cereal
- Cook a hot dog
- Put a battery in the remote control
- Cut out paper dolls
- Make a ham and cheese sandwich
- Put clean sheets on a bed
- Find a book on gold mining at the library
- Order a pizza to be delivered

Write detailed directions, explaining step by step how to do one of these tasks. Do not skip any steps, even if they are obvious. If equipment is needed, explain where to find it and how to use it.

_____

_____

_____

_____

_____

_____

_____

> To assemble, add part A to part B while holding part C upside down. Turn part D backwards while you stand on your head. Reach over your left shoulder with your right hand to attach part E which you can order for $9.99 from Timbuktu.

_____

_____

Read your directions. Are they very clear? Did you forget any steps? If you did, add them below. Draw arrows to show where they go.

_____

_____

_____

▉ WHICH WAY?

Do you think you could find your way to the bicycle repair shop by following these directions?

It's easy to get to the bicycle repair shop. Go down the street a couple of blocks. Turn by the elm tree. Keep going until you get to the house where Mr. Sanchos used to live. You can't miss it.

If you want to find a place, it's important to have clear directions to follow. How many blocks is a couple? Two? Four? Which way do you turn, right or left?

Write directions from your home or school to someplace at least a mile away. You could give directions to a park, the library, the mall, a computer store, a restaurant or someplace else. Draw a map to go with your directions.

How to get from _____ to _____

Draw your map here.

▉ COULD YOU BE MORE SPECIFIC?

How many times have you heard someone say, "Have a nice day"? What is a "nice" day? A sunny day? A day when you get presents? Your birthday? The word *nice* is very general. It could mean many things.

The more specific a writer is, the better readers will understand.

Read the sentences below. Which sentences are very general? Which sentences give you specific information?

- A car went by fast.
- A red Mustang convertible drove past at 80 miles an hour.
- The dog barked.
- When the huge brown and white St. Bernard barked, it sounded like a fog horn.

Look at the list of words below. Each one represents a general category. After each word, write a word or phrase that is more specific.

toy: _____

truck: _____

game: _____

holiday: _____

sport: _____

parade: _____

dog: _____

animal: _____

magazine: _____

video: _____

rug: _____

house: _____

child: _____

Rewrite these sentences so they are more specific.

A girl caught a fish. _____

_____

The frog made noise. _____

_____

A boy sat in a chair. _____

_____

TLC10017 Copyright © Teaching & Learning Company, Carthage, IL 62321

EXACTLY WHAT DO YOU MEAN?

What do you think of when you hear the word *hat*? A hat could be frilly with feathers. It could be a hard hat or a baseball cap. Abe Lincoln wore a top hat. When you go fishing, you might wear a fishing hat. Do any of these hats look alike?

Make your writing more interesting by telling readers what kind of hat a character is wearing. What color is it? What size and shape?

For each **bold** word, make a list of many different types of that object.

Ted rode in a **boat.**

_____

_____

_____

_____

_____

_____

I filled the **bag** to the top.

_____

_____

_____

_____

_____

_____

_____

I lost my favorite pair of **shoes.**

_____

_____

_____

_____

_____

_____

_____

I dropped the **ball.**

_____

_____

_____

_____

_____

_____

_____

▦ HELP WANTED

> Person needed to clean the bottom of shark tank. Must be fast swimmer.

When you place an ad in the classified section of a newspaper, you pay by the word. You want to include all necessary information in as few words as possible.

This ad has too many unnecessary words.

> For Sale: Beautiful old car made in 1937 by Dodge. Completely restored. Painted a lovely shade of pink. Will sell to a good home. Call 555-1212 after six at night.

Rewrite this ad in 12 words or less.

For Sale: _____

_____

_____

_____

_____   Number of words: _____

Write a HELP WANTED ad for a lion tamer in 15 words or less.

Help Wanted: _____

_____

_____

_____

_____   Number of words: _____

Write a WANTED TO BUY ad for a dog in 15 words or less.

Wanted to Buy: _____

_____

_____

_____

_____   Number of words: _____

LEAVE A MESSAGE

You're waiting for your friend in your tree house when your mother calls you and asks you to go to the store. You won't be gone long. You want to let your friend know you'll be back in a few minutes.

You look around but don't see any paper, pens, pencils, markers or crayons. The only things in the tree house are the items below. How could you use these items to leave a message for your friend?

Draw a picture to show what your message looks like.

WHAT'S YOUR ADVICE?

You write an advice column for a newspaper. How would you answer these two letters?

Dear Wise One,

Last week I picked up an old envelope on the side-walk on my way home from school. I looked inside and found a twenty dollar bill! The address on the envelope is for a town 15 miles away. What should I do?

Confused

Dear Confused,

_____

_____

_____

_____

_____

_____

_____

Dear Wise One,

I saw my best friend cheating on the math test yesterday. Our teacher didn't see it. What should I do? I don't want to make my friend mad, but I know cheating is wrong.

In need of help

Dear In need of help,

_____

_____

_____

_____

_____

_____

_____

▚ CHECK YOUR WORK

When you finish writing a story, poem or report, take time to edit it. To **edit** means to read it again very carefully and make changes that are needed.

Edit a story, poem or report you have written. Read it again very carefully, then answer the questions below to yourself. Make the necessary changes to your story, poem or report.

- Are all your facts correct? Did you mention that your character was a member of the Dallas Oilers instead of the Dallas Cowboys? Always check your facts.

- Have you included all the information needed? Did you forget to add something the reader needs to know?

- Did you include too much information? Does the reader really need to know that blue is Sara's favorite color if it has nothing to do with the story?

- Did you use strong adjectives to describe the nouns? Did you use too many adjectives?

- Were you consistent? If Tim wore a green shirt in the first paragraph, he probably shouldn't be wearing a red one in the second paragraph.

- Does your dialogue sound real? Do people really talk that way?

- Do you have a good ending? Could it be better?

- Could you use words that are more clear in some places?

Rewrite your story, poem or report with the changes you made.

How can editing help you write better? _____

_____

A PENNY SAVED IS IS A PENNY EARNED

Proofreading, also called proofing, is important to all writers. It takes a lot of work to write a story, poem, report or other assignment. Take time to look it over closely before you hand it in. To proofread means to check your writing for errors.

What to look for when you proofread:

- Does each sentence begin with a capital letter?
- Did you use complete sentences?
- Are proper nouns capitalized?
- Do subjects and verbs agree?
- Did you skip any words?
- Are all words spelled correctly?
- Did you repeat any words in a row?
- Did you use correct punctuation?

Proofread the following paragraph. Cross out each mistake and write the correction above the error.

Somebody or Nobody?

Mr. Nobody and Miss Somebody plan to to get married soon. One small problem is is stopping thrm from setting the date.

Miss Somebody wants too keep her last Name after they get married. mr. Nobody wants her to change it. He thinks she sould be Mrs Nobody. He wants they're children to be little Nobodys.

Miss Somebody likes her her last name. She wants to to be a Somebody If they have children, th girls could be Somebodys and the boys could bee Nobodys. Mr. Nobody doesn't not agree.

Miss somebody thought they culd use both names and be Mr. and Mrs. Somebody-Nobody. that ideas didn't make Mr. Nobody

happy either.

If they don't find an answer to the their problem, there won't be a wedding Maybe they should both change their last names to jones.

Go back and look at the title of this page. What's wrong with it?

KNOW YOUR CHARACTERS

It can be difficult to write about a character if you don't know the person well. Spend time getting to know your characters before you put them in a story. Look at the pictures below. One of them could be a character in your story. Write some words and phrases that tell about these people on the lines by each picture.

Name: _____ Age: _____

Nickname: _____

How did she get her nickname? _____

_____

Hair color: _____

What's her favorite color? _____

Why? _____

Favorite sport: _____

What kind of clothing does she usually wear? _____

Describe her best friend. _____

_____

Why does she like snow? _____

Name: _____ Age: _____

City she lives in: _____

Eye color: _____

What pets does she have? _____

What are her favorite games? _____

_____

What job would she like to do someday? _____

What did she do after school yesterday? _____

_____

What kind of pizza does she like? _____

Name _____

Name: _____ Age: _____

What unusual item does he collect?_____

What are his favorite foods?_____

_____

What subject does he like best in school? _____

_____

Why didn't he tell his parents about the snake he keeps in a shoe box under his bed?

_____

What will he do before school tomorrow? _____

Who is his favorite actor? Why? _____

_____

What color is his toothbrush? _____

Name: _____ Age:_____

What secret does he have?_____

_____

Why does he like porcupines? _____

_____

Why does he always wear purple socks?_____

_____

What does he do every day at 4 p.m.?_____

What's his favorite place to be alone? _____

How does he feel about computers? _____

What is his favorite holiday? _____ Why?_____

What makes him happy?_____

_____

On another sheet of paper, write a short story using two or more of these characters.

Name _____

BRING CHARACTERS TO LIFE

To make your characters "come alive," you need to know how they think, how they feel, what they like and dislike.

Below each picture, write seven words or short phrases to describe the person shown. Include two things they like and two things they dislike.

List seven words or phrases that describe this character.

_____

_____

_____

_____

_____

_____

_____

Two things she dislikes are:

_____

_____

Two things she likes are:

_____

_____

List seven words or phrases that describe this character.

_____

_____

_____

_____

_____

_____

_____

Two things he dislikes are:

_____

_____

Two things he likes are:

_____

_____

On the back of this paper, write a paragraph describing one of these people. Use the words and phrases you listed.

CLASH OF THE CHARACTERS

Good stories show **conflict**. *Conflict* means "some kind of struggle or problem that needs to be solved." It could be a problem between two people, between a person and nature or between two animals.

Conflict makes a story more interesting. Imagine reading a story about someone who got up in the morning, got dressed, ate breakfast, went to school, came home, ate supper and went to bed. BORING.

Now take that same person, on the same day and add conflict. The person could experience several types of conflicts or problems even before he or she had a chance to eat breakfast. Any one of these could be the basis for a story.

- Did he oversleep? Why?
- Did her sister wear the sweater she was planning to wear? Now what will she wear?
- Was his toast burnt? Did the toaster start on fire?
- Did she slip in the shower? Then what happened?
- Did his goldfish eat his homework? How can he prove it to his teacher?
- Did her brother put a mouse in her shoe? What will she do to him?

Think of an idea for a story that involves a type of conflict. Write a summary of your idea in one sentence.

_____

_____

_____

List at least three ways this problem might be resolved.

_____

_____

_____

_____

IT DEPENDS ON HOW YOU LOOK AT IT

How we see an event depends on our point of view. A person who saw a car and truck crash would have a different point of view than the driver of the car or the driver of the truck. Someone riding in the car might have a different point of view.

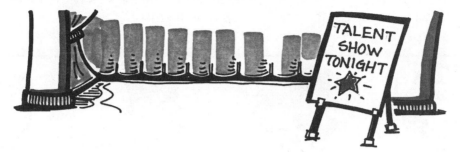

Write a short paragraph about attending the school talent show from four different points of view.

1. You will be doing a juggling act in the talent show.

    _____

    _____

    _____

    _____

2. You are a proud parent going to the show to watch your child do a juggling act.

    _____

    _____

    _____

    _____

3. You are the fourteen-year-old brother or sister of the person doing the juggling act. You'd rather be out playing baseball.

    _____

    _____

    _____

    _____

4. Select another person who will be attending the talent show, and write from his or her point of view.

    _____

    _____

    _____

Read *Freaky Friday* by Mary Rodgers.

◼ WHAT WOULD THEY SAY?

The words people speak in a story are called **dialogue**. When you write dialogue, the words should sound the way people really talk.

Look at the faces of the people below. Think about what they might say. To make dialogue sound natural, say the words out loud before you write them.

1.  2.  3.  4.

Girl 1 found a large, hairy spider under her bed. What would she say to her older sister?

_____

_____

_____

Girl 2 looked in the mirror and saw a sad face looking back. What did she say to her mirror?

_____

_____

_____

Boy 3 wasn't chosen for the football team. What did he say to his coach?

_____

_____

_____

Man 4 found a lost child crying in the park. What did he say to the child?

_____

_____

_____

On another sheet of paper, write dialogue between two of the people shown above.

■ SHOW TIME

Work with a partner to make two puppets. You could decorate small paper bags or make finger puppets. You could cut pictures of people from magazines and glue them to craft sticks.

Imagine the two puppets talking to each other. Take turns writing what they say to each other.

Puppet 1: _____

_____

_____

Puppet 2: _____

_____

_____

Puppet 1: _____

_____

_____

Puppet 2: _____

_____

_____

Puppet 1: _____

_____

_____

Puppet 2: _____

_____

_____

■ "COME INTO MY PARLOR," SAID THE SPIDER TO THE FLY

What if objects and animals could talk? What would they say? Who would they talk to? Select one pair of items. Write a conversation they might have.

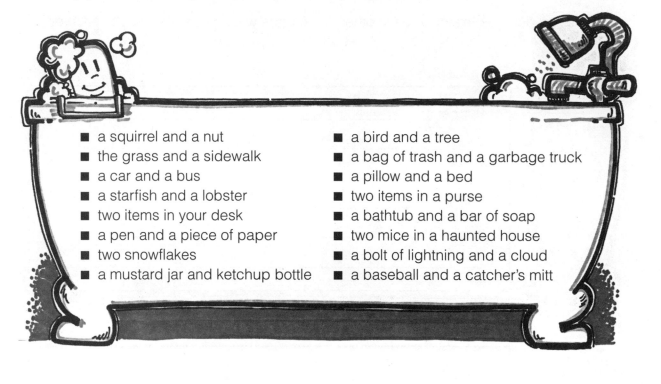

- a squirrel and a nut
- the grass and a sidewalk
- a car and a bus
- a starfish and a lobster
- two items in your desk
- a pen and a piece of paper
- two snowflakes
- a mustard jar and ketchup bottle
- a bird and a tree
- a bag of trash and a garbage truck
- a pillow and a bed
- two items in a purse
- a bathtub and a bar of soap
- two mice in a haunted house
- a bolt of lightning and a cloud
- a baseball and a catcher's mitt

_____
_____
_____
_____
_____
_____
_____
_____
_____
_____
_____
_____
_____
_____
_____

THE LITTLE DOG LAUGHED

Personification is a figure of speech that gives a human quality to something nonhuman.

The wind howled . . .   The smiling moon . . .   The cat laughed . . .

Television commercials show a tiger selling cereal, soda cans that talk and dogs and cats that complain about their supper. These are also examples of personification.

Describe three TV commercials that use personification.

1. _____

   _____

2. _____

   _____

3. _____

   _____

Fill in the blanks below with other examples of personification.

The unforgiving _____

The happy _____

The _____ laughed

The _____ day

A _____ wind

The _____ dolphin

A wise _____

You can find many examples of personification in Aesop's fables where animals think, talk and act like people. List other books or stories where authors use personification.

_____

_____

_____

_____

Read *Charlotte's Web* by E.B. White.

▓ DON'T COUNT YOUR CHICKENS BEFORE THEY HATCH

A parable is a story that teaches a lesson. Remember how the tortoise beat the hare in a race? What happened when the man killed the goose that laid the golden egg?

Write your own parable. You can select one of these lessons or choose one of your own.

- ■ Haste makes waste.
- ■ Persistence wins the race.
- ■ One good turn deserves another.
- ■ Little by little does the trick.
- ■ A rolling stone gathers no moss.
- ■ The squeaky wheel gets the attention.
- ■ Little friends may prove great friends.
- ■ It's easy to propose impossible solutions.

_____

_____

_____

_____

_____

_____

_____

_____

_____

_____

_____

Read Aesop.

WHY DO ZEBRAS HAVE STRIPES?

Scientists can explain why water is blue, why snowflakes have six sides and much more. Sometimes though, it's more fun to make up your own reason for why things are the way they are.

Select one of the questions. Make up an answer. Be as silly or creative as you can.

Where does a rainbow go?

Why do spiders have eight legs?

How do flies walk upside down?

What color is a giggle?

Why do zebras have stripes?

Why do people have ten toes?

_____

_____

_____

_____

_____

_____

_____

_____

_____

_____

_____

_____

To learn how the camel got his hump and how the leopard got his spots, read *Just So Stories* by Rudyard Kipling.

WHY DOES THE SUN RISE IN THE EAST?

Ancient people used **myths** to explain what they could not understand. Why does the sun rise every day and set every night? Why does it get cold in winter and warm in spring? How did mountains and rivers come to be? Who controls the thunder and lightning?

Write a myth to explain one of these mysteries or make up a question of your own to answer.

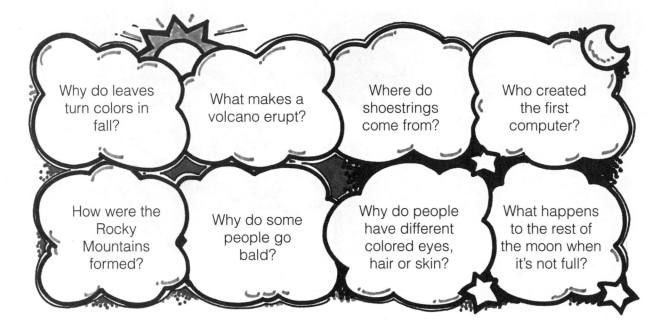

Why do leaves turn colors in fall?

What makes a volcano erupt?

Where do shoestrings come from?

Who created the first computer?

How were the Rocky Mountains formed?

Why do some people go bald?

Why do people have different colored eyes, hair or skin?

What happens to the rest of the moon when it's not full?

_____

_____

_____

_____

_____

_____

_____

_____

_____

_____

_____

_____

_____

Read some myths from other cultures.

WHAT DOES IT MEAN?

A proverb is a familiar saying that expresses some type of folk wisdom. Proverbs often have more than one meaning.

A stitch in time saves nine.

If you sew up a small hole, it won't get bigger. If you take care of any type of problem while it is small, it won't get worse.

Read these proverbs. Explain what you think they mean.

The squeaky wheel gets the grease. _____

_____

Fight fire with fire. _____

_____

Beauty is in the eye of the beholder._____

_____

Honesty pays. _____

_____

Waste not, want not._____

_____

A bird in the hand is worth two in the bush. _____

_____

Beauty is only skin deep. _____

_____

Make up your own proverb. Trade papers with a classmate. Ask your classmate to write a sentence to explain what your proverb means.

Your proverb: _____

_____

_____

_____

_____

_____

GRIZZLY BEAR DAY

According to legend, if the groundhog sees his shadow on February second, he will be frightened and run back inside to sleep. Winter will continue for six more weeks. If he doesn't see his shadow, he will come out and play. Spring will arrive soon.

Make up a story about a growly old grizzly bear or another animal who comes out in spring after sleeping all winter. What day does he come out? What will happen if he sees his shadow? What will happen if he doesn't see it?

▊ CALL ME ISHMAEL

Some stories are written in first person. In a first person story, the author tells the story from one character's point of view.

> I'm old now, but my memory of that terrible day fifty years ago hasn't faded. I remember every detail from the time I woke up early in the morning until the clock struck midnight.

When writing in first person, only the events seen, heard, thought and felt by the character telling the story can be used. How other characters felt and what they thought must be expressed through the character telling the story.

> Kayla told me she had a bad feeling when the wind started to rise. She said she knew something was about to happen.

When you write a story in first person, you become the character telling the story. Write two first person sentences below.

_____

_____

_____

_____

_____

_____

Herman Melville wrote *Moby Dick* in first person. Here are his first two sentences.

> Call me Ishmael. Some years ago—never mind how long precisely—having little or no money in my purse, and nothing particular to interest me on shore, I thought I would sail about a little and see the watery part of the world.

FROM THIRD TO FIRST

Read the following paragraph. Rewrite it in first person.

Bob rushed to the door in his pajamas. He wondered who could be making such a racket so early in the morning. He was sure it was someone with bad news. As he reached for the doorknob, he stopped. Maybe he shouldn't open the door. Maybe he should go back to bed and pretend he hadn't heard the racket. Bob took a deep breath and made his decision.

_____
_____
_____
_____
_____
_____
_____
_____
_____
_____
_____
_____

What did Bob decide to do? Write an ending to this story in first or third person.

_____
_____
_____
_____
_____
_____

ONLY A DREAM?

A noun is the name of a person, place or thing. Examples of nouns are *book, toy, umbrella, uncle, mother, park, zoo* and *circus*.

How many nouns can you find in the following story? Underline them as you read.

Only a Dream?

Amy thought she was dreaming when she opened her eyes. A dragon sat at her desk, wearing a red dress and reading a book. Amy saw the dragon very clearly in the moonlight.

At first Amy was afraid. She tried to call her parents. The only sound she could make was a small squeak.

When the dragon heard the noise, it put the book on the desk. The dragon turned and smiled at Amy in a way that only a dragon could smile. Amy knew the dragon wanted to be her friend.

Carefully, she opened the drawer in the table by her bed and took out a piece of candy. She handed it to the dragon.

The dragon took the candy very politely, put the wrapper on the desk and ate the candy.

Amy closed her eyes for a minute, while she thought about the proper way to talk to a dragon. The sound of her mother's voice made her eyes snap wide open.

"Amy, it's time to get up for school," her mother called. "Are you going to wear your new red dress today?"

Amy looked around the empty room. There was no dragon. She was disappointed. It must have been a dream. Then she saw the candy wrapper next to the book on the desk. Her red dress was folded neatly over the back of the chair. Do you think it was only a dream?

List ten other nouns not found in the story.

_____   _____

_____   _____

_____   _____

_____   _____

_____   _____

▌▌FROM A TO Z

Adjectives are words that describe a person, place or thing. Writers use adjectives to make a story more colorful and more interesting. *Big, quiet, yellow, hungry* and *tired* are adjectives.

Think of adjectives that begin with each letter of the alphabet. Write them on the lines after the letters. You can write more than one adjective for any letter. Skip around to different letters as you work. If you have trouble thinking of an adjective that begins with *X* or another letter, use a word that has that letter someplace in the word.

A _____   _____

B _____   _____

C _____   _____

D _____   _____

E _____   _____

F _____   _____

G _____   _____

H _____   _____

I _____   _____

J _____   _____

K _____   _____

L _____   _____

M _____   _____

N _____   _____

O _____   _____

P _____   _____

Q _____   _____

R _____   _____

S _____   _____

T _____   _____

U _____   _____

V _____   _____

W _____   _____

X _____   _____

Y _____   _____

Z _____   _____

▮ A DARK, STORMY NIGHT

Adjectives are words that describe people, places or things.

Underline the adjectives in the following story.

A Great Day for a Picnic

Shannon looked at the dark, cloudy sky. It's going to be a wet, gloomy day, he thought sadly. He and his three best friends had planned a big picnic at their favorite sandy beach. Shannon was bringing ham and cheese sandwiches. Marla planned to bake a fresh apple pie. Tito was bringing cherry soda and Sue Ling planned to bring ripe red strawberries. Suddenly the hot bright sun broke through and scattered the dark clouds. "Hurray," shouted Shannon. "Now we can have our picnic after all."

Look back at the A to Z list of adjectives you wrote. Use the words on your list or other adjectives to complete the phrases below.

The _____ water

A _____ child

The _____ park

A _____ puppy

The _____ lion

A _____ circus

A(n) _____ _____ balloon

Many _____ _____ trees

The smell of a _____ _____ pie

The _____ _____ movie

A(n) _____ _____ garden

A(n) _____ _____ breeze

The _____ _____ man

A(n) _____ _____ Saturday

One _____ _____ evening

A(n) _____ _____ smell

The _____ _____ thunderstorm

A(n) _____ _____ report card

▮ HOW NOW?

Adverbs are words that describe verbs (predicates). They describe **how** something was done. Many adverbs end with the letters -*ly*. *Quickly, slowly, happily* and *carefully* are adverbs.

Finish each sentence by writing an adverb in the blank. Use words from the list on the right or make up your own. You can use a word more than once.

Shanikwa walked _____	badly
	bravely
Roberto talked _____	brightly
	calmly
Jennifer ran _____	cheerfully
	clearly
Cody sailed _____	gently
	gladly
Andy jumped _____	happily
	joyfully
Paula turned _____	kindly
	loudly
Terry laughed _____	nearly
	poorly
Rosa slept _____	quickly
	quietly
James marched _____	rapidly
	rarely
Lisa danced _____	recently
	sadly
Heather called _____	slowly
	softly
Mark drove _____	soundly
	suddenly
Danika sang _____	tearfully
	weakly
Jameel read _____	wisely

Myrna spoke _____

HAPPINESS IS A PERFECT CHECKUP AT THE DENTIST'S

A metaphor is a figure of speech that compares two different objects or ideas without using the words *like* or *as*.

Write metaphors to finish the sentences. Do not use the words *like* or *as*.

Happiness is _____

Sadness is _____

Spring is _____

Excited is _____

Funny is _____

A bad day is _____

A good day is _____

Friends are _____

Life is _____

Scared is _____

Hope is _____

Rain is _____

Laughter is _____

My family is _____

Salty peanuts are _____

Tired is _____

▦ A BEARD LIKE A BIRD'S NEST

A simile is a figure of speech that compares two different objects or ideas by using the words *like* or *as*.

Josh was as timid as a turtle.
Ann's hair looked like sunshine in the wind.

Fill in the blanks to complete the following similes. You may use more than one word to complete the sentences.

He saw a snake as large as _____.

Barry was as happy as_____.

Cora's eyes looked like the eyes of _____.

Don's voice was as sweet as_____.

The waterfall sounded like_____.

The rain fell as fast as_____.

Frank's voice sounded like _____.

Gina felt as scared as _____.

When Misha saw the gorilla, he ran as fast as_____.

Justin thought the train whistle sounded like _____.

Kym drank the sour milk. It tasted like _____.

Lynn found an apple as large as _____.

On her birthday, Juanita received a gift as special as _____.

Stacy's clothes were as colorful as _____.

Write similes of your own on the lines below.

_____

_____

_____

_____

_____

_____

_____

◼◼▦ TREASURE HUNT

You and a friend followed a treasure map to the spot marked with an *X*. You are hot and sweaty after digging for hours. Suddenly, you find a large chest. You and your friend open it and find something unusual. It isn't gold, coins or jewels.

Complete the picture to show what you found in the treasure chest. On the lines below, describe what you found and how you felt.

◼️◼️ SEA HUNT

Imagine going down, down to the bottom of the ocean in a submarine. Look around. Describe what you see and how it makes you feel.

PAINT A WORD PICTURE

Some artists paint beautiful pictures. So do some writers. Writers paint their pictures with words.

A rose

A yellow rose in a vase

A faded yellow rose in a cracked coffee mug

Which description of the rose paints the clearest picture?

Paint word pictures of your own. Use words that describe the color, smell, sound, taste and feel of the object.

A loaf of bread: _____

_____

Sandpaper: _____

_____

The midway at a circus: _____

_____

A daisy: _____

_____

A drop of rain: _____

_____

A snowflake: _____

_____

An ice-cream cone: _____

_____

▚ BUY ME

Ads encourage people to buy a product or use the services of a business. Magazine and newspaper ads use words and pictures. Television ads combine words with sound and pictures.

What is your favorite ad? _____

Why? _____

_____

_____

Think about other ads. How are color, scenery, celebrities, cartoon characters and "catch" words used?

People associate catch words or slogans with certain products.

    Golden arches . . .

    "Things go better with . . ."

    ". . . melt in your mouth, not in your hands."

Cut out an ad from a newspaper or magazine. Tape it to the back of this page. Study it carefully.

1. How are words used in the ad to appeal to the reader?

   _____

2. What slogan or "catch" words are associated with this product?

   _____

3. How are pictures and colors used to make the product appealing?

   _____

   _____

4. If a celebrity or cartoon character appears in the ad, how does he or she promote the product?

   _____

◼▦ WHY BUY SPINACH ICE CREAM?

You work for an ice cream company. It's your job to design a magazine ad for a new product: spinach-flavored ice cream. Hurry, one million gallons will be sent out to the stores next week.

You need an appealing name for the product. What will you call it?

_____

_____

To help people remember your product, write a slogan for it.

_____

_____

What words will you use in the magazine ad to convince people to buy this product?

_____

_____

_____

_____

Draw or describe the picture to go with the ad in the box below.

BUCKLE UP

Ads can convince people to buy a product, shop at a certain store or fly on an airline. Ads can also sell an idea.

Ads to sell an idea are like ads to sell a product. They use words, pictures, music and slogans.

- "Buckle Up" reminds people to use their seat belts.
- Smokey Bear tells people, "Only you can prevent forest fires."
- A friendly owl says, "Give a hoot. Don't pollute."

Select one of the topics below. Write a slogan to convince people to . . .

- carpool to work
- vote on election day
- be more patriotic
- get more exercise
- protect an endangered species
- read more books
- wear bicycle helmets
- conserve water
- recycle

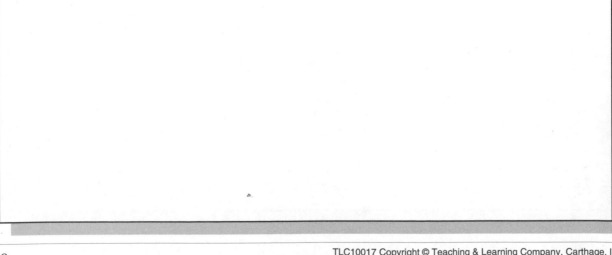

Write a slogan to sell your idea. _____

_____

_____

Draw or describe a celebrity or cartoon character to be the spokesperson for your ideas in the box below.

BUCKLE UP

◼ VOTE FOR VINCE

Ad writers help people running for office. They design ads that catch people's attention and convince them to vote for the candidate. The words, pictures and music are carefully chosen. A slogan may be used to help voters remember the person's name.

Imagine yourself running for office. What office would you like to be elected to fill? You can use a real one or make one up.

_____

Write a slogan for yourself. _____

_____

_____

Write a one-minute radio ad to convince people to vote for you. Write the words for the ad. Describe the background music you will use.

_____

_____

_____

_____

_____

_____

_____

_____

_____

_____

_____

_____

_____

_____

_____

WORDS THAT AREN'T BUT SHOULD BE

Sometimes authors make up words. In his book *The Lorax*, Dr. Seuss uses made-up words like *snergelly, snarggled, smogulous, glumping* and *smoke-smuggered*.

Make up your own words to describe these situations:

How you feel when you're snug and warm on a cold winter night:

_____

The sound of a flat tire:

_____

The way your mouth feels in the morning before you brush your teeth:

_____

The smell of a gym locker on a hot summer day:

_____

The feel of sandpaper:

_____

The taste of cotton candy:

_____

A large bite of a juicy lemon:

_____

Make up words of your own and list them below. Explain what they mean.

My Made-Up Words	What They Mean
_____	_____
_____	_____
_____	_____
_____	_____
_____	_____

Read *The Lorax* or other books by Dr. Seuss. Look for examples of made-up words. Try to figure out what his made-up words mean. Read *Jabberwocky* by Lewis Carroll.

▊ A MILLION TIMES

Has anyone ever said to you, "I've told you a million times not to slam the door." Did the person really mean a million times or was she exaggerating? A **hyperbole** is a figure of speech that is an extreme exaggeration of the truth.

- I'm hungry enough to eat a horse.
- I thought I'd die from embarrassment.
- I waited forever for you to show up.

Finish the sentences with hyperboles. Remember to exaggerate.

Molly ran as fast as _____

Alicia was so embarrassed _____

Josh was so tall he could _____

For breakfast, Paul Bunyan ate _____

I laughed so hard _____

The mess in my room was as big as _____

The snake was as long as a _____

I worked so hard _____

The pothole was so big _____

The line at the movie was as long as _____

Jessie walked so slowly _____

The bus was so crowded _____

I caught a fish the size of a _____

I was so tired I could have slept _____

Tasha was so cold _____

The room was hot enough to _____

John Henry worked so hard _____

Pecos Bill tamed a wild horse as big as _____

SUPER SNAIL TO THE RESCUE

Have you ever read about Paul Bunyan, John Henry or Pecos Bill? Have you ever seen the Teenage Mutant Ninja Turtles? These characters are "superheroes" with special skills.

> Paul Bunyan, a lumberjack, roamed the northern U.S. with Babe, a huge Blue Ox. Babe used to get mighty thirsty. Paul scooped out lots of big holes. The holes filled with water and Babe had plenty to drink. That's why Wisconsin has 15,000 lakes!

Your superhero could be a man, woman, animal, plant or alien. The hero could be very tall or very small, super strong or extra smart. Superheroes always have very special talents.

Describe your superhero. Use lots of hyperboles to describe your superhero. She could be tall enough to reach clouds, smarter than a computer or able to become invisible. Your superhero could be stronger than a grizzly bear, able to rope a thunder cloud and ride it across the sky or hungry enough to eat fourteen extra-large deluxe supreme pizzas as a bedtime snack.

Hero's name: _____

Height and weight: _____

Special skills or talents: _____

Tools or equipment used: _____

Where does your hero live?_____

What does your hero wear? _____

What makes your hero laugh? _____

What makes your hero sad? _____

What great task did your hero do?_____

Describe your hero's pets or special friends. _____

_____

How did this person become a superhero?_____

_____

Other important information about your superhero: _____

_____

Write a short story about an adventure your superhero had.

On the back of this page, draw a picture of your superhero.

RHYME TIME

Many poems use words that rhyme. Words like *dog, cat* and *sad* are easy to rhyme. Words like *elephant, telephone* and *motorcycle* are more difficult. Sometimes poets make up words that rhyme.

When you rhyme words of two or more syllables, you can rhyme the whole word: Willie, silly, frilly—or just the last syllable: bee, tree, me, see.

Write as many rhymes as you can for the words below. You can add made-up words if you like.

car _____   hill _____

_____   _____

_____   _____

ant _____   today _____

_____   _____

_____   _____

went _____   bear _____

_____   _____

_____   _____

banana _____   ocean _____

_____   _____

_____   _____

whale _____   pretty _____

_____   _____

_____   _____

ONE, TWO, BUCKLE MY SHOE

A couplet is two lines of a poem that rhyme. A couplet can be part of a longer poem. The nursery rhyme "One, Two, Buckle My Shoe" is written in couplets.

The first two lines of a limerick are a couplet. So are the third and fourth lines. Sometimes a couplet can be the entire poem.

Read the first line of each couplet below. Think of words that rhyme with the last word. Then write the second line. The last word in line two must rhyme with the last word or syllable in line one.

I met a friend at the mall today

_____

I live in a house at the top of a hill

_____

In the evening when I go to bed

_____

My favorite food is a crisp salty pickle

_____

The penguins danced in the bright moonlight

_____

Late last night I had a dream

_____

In winter when the North wind blows

_____

Raindrops glisten on my windowpane

_____

Write your own couplet.

_____

_____

◨ THE TENNESSEE FAIR

Limericks are five-line poems that are fun to read and write. The subject is usually not anything serious.

- ■ Lines 1, 2 and 5 rhyme.
- ■ Lines 3 and 4 rhyme and are shorter.

These two limericks could be sung to the tune of "The Animal Fair."

Tennessee Fair

I went to the Tennessee fair.
The horses and sheep were there.
An old raccoon,
By the light of the moon
Was combing his curly hair.

The cockatoo was blue.
He wore a bright green shoe.
The parakeet said,
"Your shoes should be red
'Cause green doesn't look good on you."

Write a limerick using the same melody. Pattern it after the one above.

I went to _____

The _____

_____

_____

_____

Rewrite your limerick until you have it the way you want it. Read or sing it to your friends. Write your final copy below. Don't forget to add a title.

_____

_____

_____

_____

_____

_____

THE OLD MAN WITH A BEARD

Many limericks follow a pattern used by the poet, Edward Lear. The first line of this type of limerick introduces a person.

- There was a young lady named Ann

- There was an old man from New York

Edward Lear wrote many limericks in this style. Here's one example:

The Old Man with a Beard

There was an old man with a beard
Who said, "It is just as I feared!
Two owls and a wren
Two larks and a hen,
Have all made a nest in my beard!"

Edward Lear often used the last word of line one as the last word of line five. Read other limericks by Edward Lear for more examples.

Write a limerick about a person.

There was a(n) _____

Who _____

_____

_____

_____

Rewrite your limerick until you have it the way you want it. Write your final copy below. Add a title.

_____

There was a(n) _____

Who _____

_____

_____

_____

◼ SING A SILLY SONG

Many songs are poems set to music. You can write a new song by making up words for a song you know.

Are You Hungry?

Are you hungry?
Are you hungry?
Mary Lou,
Mary Lou,
Would you like some supper?
Would you like some supper?
How about pizza?
How about pizza?

Now it's your turn. Rewrite the words to the tune of "Are You Sleeping?"

Are you _____?
Are you _____?
_____,
_____,
_____
_____
_____
_____

Can you think of another verse for this song? Write it on the back of this page.

Instead of "Row, Row, Row Your Boat," what about "Drive, Drive, Drive Your Car . . ." "Fly, Fly, Fly Your Plane . . ."?

Name another song. _____

Write new words for one verse.

_____
_____
_____
_____

WHAT'S THAT NOISE?

squeak   squish

creak   shhhh   whoosh

clank   achoo   buzzzzz

A word or group of words that imitates a sound is called **onomatopoeia**. In his poem, "The Bells," Edgar Allen Poe writes about the "tintinnabulation" of the bells. Does tintinnabulation sound like ringing bells?

Write words or groups of words that imitate the sounds listed below. You can use real words or made-up words.

The sound of the wind on a dark cold night: _____

The sound when you pull the plug in a bathtub or sink: _____

The sound of a ripe apple falling from a tree: _____

The sound of a rotten apple falling from a tree: _____

The sound of a sneeze in a hollow log: _____

The sound of rain on a metal roof:_____

The sound of happy people: _____

The sound of a cactus when it rains: _____

The sound of a porcupine laughing:_____

Write your own sound words and tell what they describe.

The Word	What It Describes
_____	The sound of _____
_____	The sound of _____
_____	The sound of _____
_____	The sound of _____
_____	The sound of _____
_____	The sound of _____

WEE WILLIE WINKIE

Alliteration is the use of several words beginning with the same letter or sound.

■ The west wind whistled weirdly . . .
■ A cool, creamy chocolate cone . . .
■ Tammy taught two turtles to tango.

Fill in the blanks with words that begin with the same letter or sound as the first ones.

Red, round r_____

Wendy w_____

Big b_____ b_____

C_____ clocks

D_____ danced d_____

Freddy found f_____ f_____

A g_____ giraffe

Two t_____ t_____ toured t_____

Write your own alliterations. Pick any letter of the alphabet. Write six to ten words that begin with that letter.

_____

_____

Use the words you listed above to write a sentence. Most words in the sentence should begin with the same letter.

_____

_____

_____

Write titles for three poems. Use alliteration in your titles.

_____

_____

_____

A SIGN OF SPRING

Haiku poetry originated in Japan. Each poem consists of three, unrhymed lines. Each line has a specific number of syllables:

- ■ Line 1 = 5 syllables
- ■ Line 2 = 7 syllables
- ■ Line 3 = 5 syllables

Many haiku poems are written about nature or one of the four seasons. Here is an example.

A Sign of Spring

Two lonely robins,
Shivering. Searching through March
For a sign of spring.

Count the number of syllables in each line.

Two lone-ly rob-ins

1   2   3   4   5

Shiv-er-ing. Search-ing through March

1   2   3   4   5   6   7

For a sign of spring.

1   2   3   4   5

Which season would you like to write about? _____

Write words about the season you could use in your poem.

_____

_____

_____

Work on scrap paper to start your haiku poem. Choose your words carefully. Every syllable counts. Rewrite your poem as many times as you need to until you are satisfied with it. Count the number of syllables in each line. When you're finished, write your poem below. Don't forget the title.

_____

_____

_____

_____

DINOSAURS

Haiku poetry is often written about nature. The poems are always three lines long and have a specific number of syllables in each line.

- Line 1 = 5 syllables
- Line 2 = 7 syllables
- Line 3 = 5 syllables

Read this haiku poem about dinosaurs.

Dinosaurs once ruled
The Earth as masters of all.
Today they are dust.

Count the number of syllables in each line.

Write a title for the poem. _____

Select something in nature you would like to write about. It could be a wild animal or a pet, the wind, rain or snow. You could write about a plant or a tree, a forest, a jungle or an ocean.

Your topic: _____

Write words about your topic you might use in a haiku poem.

_____

_____

_____

_____

Work on scrap paper to start your haiku poem. Rewrite your poem as many times as you need to until you are satisfied with it. Count the number of syllables in each line. When you're finished, write your poem below. Don't forget the title.

_____

_____

_____

_____

A POEM IN FIVE LINES

A cinquain is a five-line, nonrhyming poem. There are several ways to write cinquains. One type of cinquain uses specific types of words in each line.

Sneakers

Sneakers

Stinky, worn

Jumping, climbing, exploring

Through fields and puddles

Tennies

Title

Line 1: A noun

Line 2: Two adjectives to describe the noun

Line 3: Three "ing" verbs that show action

Line 4: A short statement about line 3

Line 5: A noun that is another word for the noun in line 1

Follow the format shown above for each line. Write a cinquain of your own.

Title _____

Line 1 _____

Line 2 _____

Line 3 _____

Line 4 _____

Line 5 _____

Go back and read your poem. What words could you change to make it better? Make as many changes as you'd like on the first copy. Then rewrite your poem on the lines below.

_____

_____

_____

_____

_____

TLC10017 Copyright © Teaching & Learning Company, Carthage, IL 62321

OTHER WAYS TO WRITE CINQUAINS

Some cinquains use a certain number of syllables on each line.

Type 1: Line 1—Two syllables
Line 2—Four syllables
Line 3—Six syllables
Line 4—Eight syllables
Line 5—Two syllables

Some cinquains use a certain number of words on each line.

Type 2: Line 1—1 word
Line 2—2 words
Line 3—3 words
Line 4—4 words
Line 5—1 word

Each line has a specific purpose.

Line 1—Introduces the poem and may be the title.
Line 2—Describes the title.
Line 3—Shows action.
Line 4—Shows feeling.
Line 5—A summary which relates to the first line.

■ Example of Type 1

Books

Books are
Invitations
To enter and explore
Treasures of the past and future.
Today.

■ Example of Type 2

Books

Books
Are invitations
To explore life
Present, past and future
Mysteries.

Select a topic for a cinquain. Use one of the types shown above. Prewrite your poem on scrap paper. When you are satisfied with how it sounds, write the final copy below.

_____

_____

_____

_____

_____

_____

■ A STORY POEM

A narrative poem tells a story. It may be a simple story like "The Old Woman Who Lived in a Shoe" or a longer poem like "Casey at the Bat."

A narrative poem could be about an actual event that happened or about an event that you make up.

What event or story could you write as a narrative poem?

_____

_____

_____

_____

_____

Write words and phrases you might use in your narrative poem to tell the story.

_____

_____

_____

_____

_____

_____

Write your narrative poem here.

_____

_____

_____

_____

_____

_____

_____

_____

A POEM FROM A WORD

Acrostic poems begin with a word written down the page in capital letters, like this:

R
O
S
E
S

The word you write first is the title of the poem. The first word on line 1 begins with an *R*. The first word on line 2 begins with an *O* and so on.

Roses

R ed roses with
O vergrown thorns
S cent the air
E very
S ummer.

The lines do not have to rhyme. They do not have to contain a certain number of words or syllables.

Write a short acrostic poem for the word *pets*.

Pets

P _____

E _____

T _____

S _____

Think of a word you could use for another acrostic poem. Write the letters of the word vertically on the lines below. Then finish your poem. Rewrite until you are satisfied with it. The title of the poem will be the word you first wrote.

_____

____ _____

____ _____

____ _____

____ _____

____ _____

____ _____

VISUAL POEMS

Some poets write **concrete poems**. These poems aren't written in cement, but they do look very different from most poems. Concrete poems are written in the shape of the subject of the poem. On the right is an example.

See how the word *sunshine* is used to form a circle. The rays of the sun could be words or phrases like *flowers grow, picnics, swimming* or *summer*. Write "sunny" words around the circle to form the rays of the sun.

Write a concrete poem of your own.

Decide on a topic. _____

Decide on a shape. _____

Prewrite: What words will you use in your poem?

_____

_____

_____

_____

Title of your poem: _____

Write (draw) your poem on the bottom of this page. You could use different colored pencils to write words in your poem.

DOODLE A POEM

Fill the box below with doodles, lines and shapes. Do not try to make a specific picture. Relax and doodle for a few minutes.

Take a look at your doodles. What do you see? Do you recognize any objects? Write a short, free verse poem about what you see in your doodles or about what you were thinking about while you doodled. Relax and write a doodle poem.

▐▐▐ WANDER A WHILE

What do you think of when you hear the word *laugh*? A sound? A happy event? A babbling brook? What about the word *fish*?

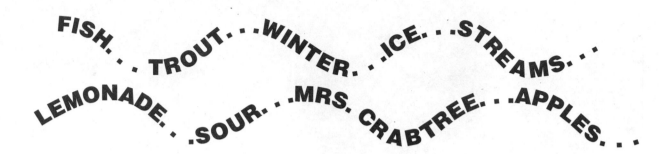

FISH. . . . TROUT. . .WINTER. . .ICE. . .STREAMS. . .
LEMONADE. . . .SOUR. . .MRS. CRABTREE. . .APPLES. . .

Start with one word. Let your mind relax. What does the first word make you think of? Follow that thought and keep going. It may take you along a strange path. Best of all, you never know where you may end up.

Letting your mind wander from one word to another, from one thought to another is called free association. Sometimes poets use this as a warm-up exercise before writing a poem.

Select a word. _____

What does that word make you think of? _____

_____

Keep going, writing any words that come to mind . . .

A HUNTING WE WILL GO

Have you ever gone hunting or fishing? Did you catch anything? Let's capture an animal but not with a trap, a hook or a gun. We'll catch it with words and keep it in a poem.

Poems can be about any animal—a whale or a mosquito, an elephant or a tadpole. You can even write about an imaginary animal.

What animal would you like to capture in a poem?

This will be a free verse poem, one that doesn't need to rhyme. Write words to describe the animal. How does it look, feel, smell? How do you feel when you think about this animal? What characteristics does this animal have? What does it eat? Where does it live?

_____

_____

_____

_____

_____

First draft: Put the words you wrote into short phrases. Move the words and phrases around. Try different combinations.

_____

_____

_____

_____

_____

Write your poem: Use the words and phrases above to write your final poem. Title your poem.

_____

_____

_____

_____

_____

▊ TREES

What words come to mind when you think of a tree? Write them below.

Select one type of tree. _____

How does it look in spring? _____

_____

In summer? _____

_____

In fall? _____

_____

In winter? _____

_____

What birds and animals live in that tree? _____

_____

How do people get pleasure from that tree? _____

_____

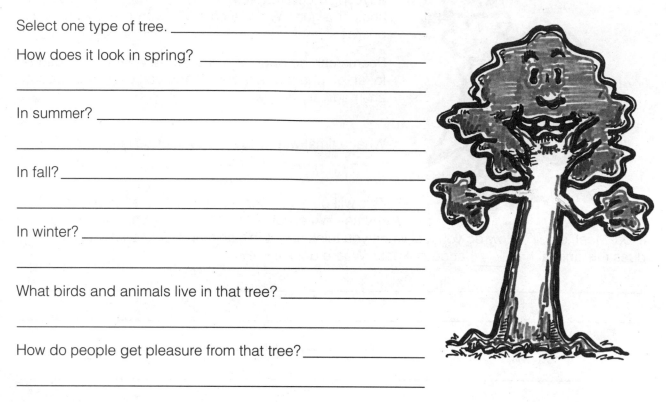

Use all of your ideas to write a poem about a tree. Try to add some similes or metaphors to your poem.

_____

_____

_____

_____

_____

_____

_____

_____

_____

Write the final copy of your poem on another sheet of paper. Draw your tree next to your poem or write the poem in the tree.

▋ A POEM ABOUT . . .

Read the list of nouns below. Any of these people, places or things could be the subject of a poem.

pumpkin	clock	shoes
supper	garbage	cocoa
mosquito	hands	window
book	school	hammer
birdhouse	butterfly	moon
rivers	parents	brothers
sisters	shoelaces	bicycle
candy	dragon	computer
mirror	steps	glasses
spring	holidays	sunset
baseball	dinosaurs	birthdays

Add fifteen or twenty more nouns (people, places or things) that you could write a poem about.

_____ _____ _____ _____

_____ _____ _____ _____

_____ _____ _____ _____

_____ _____ _____ _____

_____ _____ _____ _____

Circle the word you will use for your poem.

Write your poem below.

_____

_____

_____

_____

_____

_____

◨ AN ACTION POEM

Poems can be about something you do. Read the list of action words and phrases that could be used for a poem.

riding a bicycle	swimming	hiking
being sick	camping	sailing
choosing a gift	crying	dancing
moving to a new house	working	giggling
raking leaves	sneezing	yawning
walking on a beach	jumping	singing
playing a game	shivering	skipping
shoveling snow	tickling	hiding
writing a poem	sleeping	buying new shoes

Make a list of other action words and phrases that you could write a poem about.

_____ _____ _____ _____

_____ _____ _____ _____

_____ _____ _____ _____

_____ _____ _____ _____

Circle the words you will use for your poem.

Write your poem here.

_____

_____

_____

_____

_____

_____

THE SUNSHINE OF MY LIFE

A metaphor is a figure of speech that compares two different objects or ideas without using the words *like* or *as*.

You are my sunshine.
My sister is a monkey.
Life is a bowl of cherries.

Write two short metaphors.

_____

_____

Metaphors can be written in the form of a poem.

I am a stone,
Cold and alone.
No one notices me.

I am a robin,
Singing joyfully
On the first day of spring.

Write two metaphors comparing yourself to an animal or nonliving object. Remember, do not use the words *like* or *as* in your comparison.

I am a _____

_____

I am a _____

_____

Write a metaphor in the form of a poem.

_____

_____

_____

A FEW OF MY FAVORITE THINGS

List poems are exactly what they sound like—a list of items related in some way.

> I prefer pepperoni pizza,
> Poodles, parades,
> Pink petunias
> And purple pansies.

What would be a good title for this poem?

_____

This list poem uses alliteration (most of the words begin with the letter *P*). You can use alliteration if you'd like, but it isn't necessary. The words don't have to rhyme. You don't need a certain number of words or syllables in each line.

You can write a list poem about things you like about a person or a pet. You could list things you do on a certain day or during a certain season. Foods, flowers, people, places or animals found in a marsh are other topics for a list poem.

What are other things you could write a list poem about?

_____

_____

_____

Use scrap paper to prewrite your list poem. Rewrite it as many times as you need to until you are satisfied with it. Write the final copy of your list poem below. Don't forget the title.

_____

_____

_____

_____

_____

_____

_____

_____

◧ A GIFT THAT KEEPS ON GIVING

Want to give someone the perfect gift? Want to give a present that won't cost any money? How about writing a gift poem for someone special?

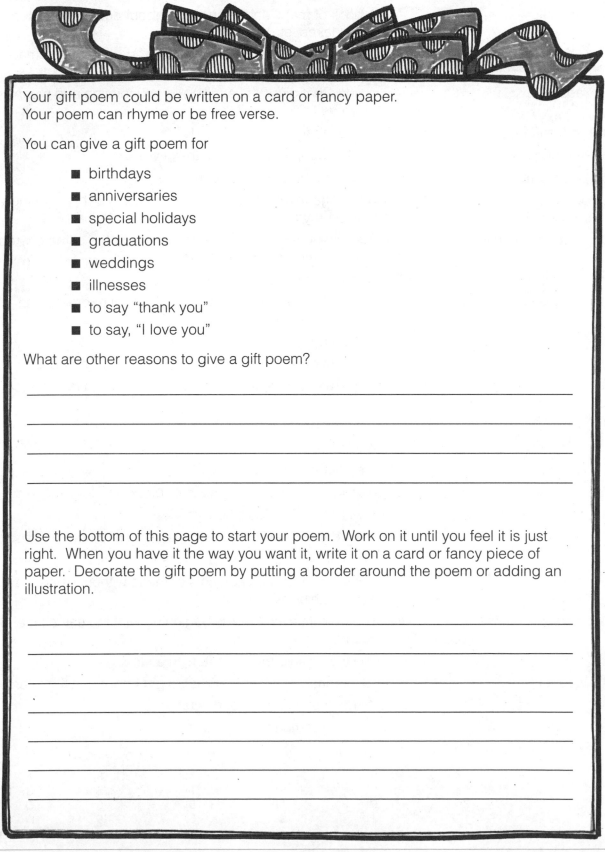

Your gift poem could be written on a card or fancy paper.
Your poem can rhyme or be free verse.

You can give a gift poem for

- birthdays
- anniversaries
- special holidays
- graduations
- weddings
- illnesses
- to say "thank you"
- to say, "I love you"

What are other reasons to give a gift poem?

_____

_____

_____

_____

Use the bottom of this page to start your poem. Work on it until you feel it is just right. When you have it the way you want it, write it on a card or fancy piece of paper. Decorate the gift poem by putting a border around the poem or adding an illustration.

_____

_____

_____

_____

_____

_____

_____

VOCABULARY REVIEW

Match the words in column 1 with the definitions in column 2.

1.	acrostic	A	A book of maps and information about countries, states, cities, lakes, etc.
2.	adjective	B	A book that contains current facts and general information on many subjects
3.	adverb	C	A book that gives the spelling, pronunciation and meaning of words
4.	alliteration	D	A book that lists similar words
5.	almanac	E	A diary people keep about their lives
6.	antonyms	F	A five-line nonrhyming poem
7.	atlas	G	A five-line rhyming poem. Lines 1, 2 and 5 rhyme. Lines 3 and 4 rhyme
8.	autobiography	H	A follow-up, as in a book or movie about the same characters at a later date
9.	biography	I	A lesson learned from a story
10.	cinquain	J	A letter to a newspaper or magazine that expresses an opinion
11.	dialogue	K	A meeting to learn more about someone
12.	dictionary	L	A nonrhyming poem with three lines and 17 syllables
13.	editorial	M	A poem that uses the first letters of a word to begin each line
14.	haiku	N	A story about someone other than the author
15.	interview	O	A story about yourself
16.	journal	P	A story that teaches a lesson
17.	limerick	Q	A word that describes a noun or pronoun
18.	metaphor	R	A word that imitates a sound
19.	moral	S	A word that modifies verbs, adjectives or other adverbs
20.	onomatopoeia	T	Attributing human characteristics to animals
21.	parable	U	Compares two unlike objects or ideas without using the words *like* or *as*
22.	personification	V	The use of several words beginning with the same letter or sounds
23.	predict	W	The words said by characters in a story
24.	sequel	X	To forecast or determine what might happen in the future
25.	synonyms	Y	Words that mean the opposite
26.	thesaurus	Z	Words that mean the same

Answers

1. M	5. B	9. N	13. J	17. G	21. P	25. Z
2. Q	6. Y	10. F	14. L	18. U	22. T	26. D
3. S	7. A	11. W	15. K	19. I	23. X	
4. V	8. O	12. C	16. E	20. R	24. H	

TLC10017 Copyright © Teaching & Learning Company, Carthage, IL 62321

BIBLIOGRAPHY

Writing Skills:

Berry, Marilyn. *help is on the way for: Book Reports* (Children's Press, 1984).

Berry, Marilyn. *help is on the way for: Writing Skills* (Children's Press, 1986).

Berry, Marilyn. *help is on the way for: Written Reports* (Children's Press, 1984).

Capacchione, Lucia. *The Creative Journal for Children* (Shambhala, 1989).

Cosman, Anna. *How to Read and Write Poetry* (Franklin Watts, 1979).

Livingston, Myra Cohn. *Poem-Making* (HarperCollins, 1991).

Tchudi, Susan and Stephen. *The Young Writer's Handbook* (Charles Scribner's Sons, 1984).

Terban, Marvin. *Funny You Should Ask: How to Make Up Jokes and Riddles with Wordplay* (Clarion Books, 1992).

Fiction:

Aesop. *Aesop's Fables* (Viking, 1981).

Andersen, Hans Christian. *The Ugly Duckling.* Retold and illustrated by Lorinda B. Cauley (Harcourt, 1979).

Blair, Walter. *Tall Tale America* (Coward, 1944).

Bowman, James C. *Pecos Bill* (Albert Whitman, 1964).

Darling, Kathy. *Pecos Bill Finds a Horse* (Garrard, 1979).

D'Aulaire, Ingri, and Edgar P. *D'Aulaires' Book of Greek Myths* (Doubleday, 1962).

Keats, Ezra John. *John Henry: An American Legend* (Pantheon, 1965).

Kipling, Rudyard. *Just So Stories* (Rand McNally, 1982).

North American Legends. Edited by Virginia Haviland (Philomel, 1979).

Paul Bunyan. Retold by Steven Kellogg (Morrow, 1984).

Rounds, Glen. *Ol' Paul: The Mighty Logger* (Morrow, 1984).

Sierra, Judy, and Robert Kaminski. *Multicultural Folktales: Stories to Tell Young Children* (Oryx Press, 1991).

Stoutenburg, Adrien. *American Tall Tales* (Viking, 1968).

Poetry Collections:

A Book of Animal Poems. Selected by William Cole (Viking, 1973).

A Few Flies and I. Haiku verses selected by Jean Merril and Ronni Solbert (Pantheon Books, 1969).

Bodecker, N.M. *Hurry, Hurry, Mary Dear! And Other Nonsense* (Atheneum, 1979).

Cricket Songs: Japanese Haiku. Translated by Harry Behn (Harcourt, 1964).

Froman, Robert. *Street Poems* (McCall, 1971).

Giroux, Joan. *The Haiku Form* (Charles E. Tuttle Company, 1974).

How to Eat a Poem and Other Morsels. Selected by Rose Agree (Pantheon Books, 1967).

Lear, Edward. *How Pleasant to Know Mr. Lear!* (Holiday House, 1972).

My Tang's Tungled and Other Ridiculous Situations. Compiled by Sara Brewton (Crowell, 1973).

Oxford Book of Poetry for Children. Edited by Edward Bilshen (Watts, 1963).

The Trees Stand Shining: Poetry of the North American Indian. Selected by Hettie Jones (Dial, 1971).

Tripp, Wallace. *A Great Big Ugly Man Came Up and Tied His Horse to Me: A Book of Nonsense Verse* (Little, 1973).

TEACHER NOTES: WRITING PROSE

As you guide students through the writing process, encourage them to try unusual approaches and solutions, to stretch their imaginations and be creative. A variety of activities ensures continuing interest and growth in young writers.

All About Me (p. 1), This Is Your Life (p. 2) and Long, Long Ago (p. 3)

Professional writers always advise young writers to write about what they know best. What subject do students know the most about? Themselves, of course.

In these two activities, students write two different types of autobiographical essays. Students describe an important personal event in **All About Me**.

They explore their feelings and write about events that caused those emotions in **This Is Your Life**. Then they express their feelings in words and pictures.

Long, Long Ago encourages students to think back to their earliest memories. Invite students to share their memories with the class.

Vocabulary word: autobiography

Dear Journal (p. 4)

Getting into the journaling habit can be a wonderful way to encourage daily writing. Journaling provides an opportunity for students to express their feelings and thoughts and spend time in self-reflection on a regular basis.

Read excerpts from *The Diary of Anne Frank* as an example of a diary that has become world famous.

Students don't need fancy books for their journals. Inexpensive spiral notebooks work fine. Give students 10 to 15 minutes every day to add to their journals. Have a list of ideas ready for those who can't think of anything to write about. You'll find many suggestions in *The Creative Journal for Children: A Guide for Parents, Teachers and Counselors*.

Assure students that their journals will be private and confidential. If they fear someone else will read their journals, they will not be honest. Journaling provides practice in writing without criticism from others.

Students can keep their journals in their desks or lockers, or you can offer to keep them in a locked drawer or cabinet. Even if you're strongly tempted to read what students write in their journals, don't betray their trust.

Vocabulary words: diary, journal, journaling

The Whole Story (p. 5)

Stories must have a beginning, a middle and an ending to be complete. Students are asked to read a short story and answer questions about these three parts of a story. For this activity you could assign a specific story or allow students to select any one they choose.

Once upon a Time (p. 6), Tale of a Peacock (p. 7) and A Large Purple Dragon Did What? (p.8)

Sometimes the most difficult part about writing is deciding what to write about. These three activities help students start a story.

Once upon a Time encourages students to look at how authors begin their stories. They are introduced to the idea that the first sentence of a story should capture the interest of the reader.

When you hand out the worksheets **Tale of a Peacock** and **A Large Purple Dragon Did What?** ask students to fold the page at the solid line and complete the directions on the top of the page. When they have finished, they can continue the activity. These two activities help students begin a story by giving them a first sentence based on a random selection of numbers. With 10,000 possible combinations on each worksheet, it is doubtful that any two students will begin their stories with the same first sentence.

Once students have chosen the four parts of their beginning sentences, be certain they know the meaning of every word in the sentence. Have dictionaries available in case they're needed.

Vocabulary words: fiction, creative

One, Two Three, Let's Write Together (p. 9)

This cooperative activity encourages teamwork as students practice writing beginnings, middles and endings for short stories. If students have trouble getting started, they could go back to **A Large Purple Dragon Did What?** and **Tale of a Peacock** for ideas.

Repeat the activity several times to give students practice in all three stages of storytelling. Encourage students to read their stories to the class. Ask the student who wrote the first sentence to compare how he or she expected a story to end with how it actually did end.

Designing a Plan (p. 10) and Building a Story (p. 11)

These two activities are designed to be used sequentially. Students are asked to plan and "build" a story for younger children. Using several sheets of typing paper folded in half and stapled together, students could transfer their story to a "book" complete with colorful illustrations.

Invite a group of kindergarten or first grade students to your class for story time. Divide the visitors into small groups. Assign two students to each group of visitors to read their stories out loud.

The Rest of the Story (p. 12)

Students receive additional help starting a story in this activity. They select a starting sentence and continue the story line to complete a story of their own.

Have two students who used the same first sentence read their stories to the class. Ask the class to compare how the stories are alike and how they are different. Encourage positive comments about both stories, even if one is clearly better than the other.

To write another group story, read one of the beginning sentences from this activity to the class. Let students take turns adding one sentence to the story. Tape your class story as they tell it and play it back for them.

Part Two (p.13)

Before starting this activity, discuss movies and books students have seen and read that have sequels. Have any of the students read series like the Hardy Boys or the Babysitter Club? What was their reaction?

This activity could be used with a specific reading assignment. In a class discussion, encourage students to ask questions about characters that aren't answered at the end of a story.

Vocabulary words: sequel, character

Write from Experience (p. 14)

Young writers are advised to write from their experiences. They can use past experiences to project themselves into new situations. This activity encourages students to take an inventory of their experiences.

Encourage students in other "writing from experience" activities. They could write about a dream, a memory or the first time they had an experience (tasted an usual food, went to the hospital, went skiing, saw a monkey . . .).

Get to Know Someone (p. 15) and The Life and Times of Someone Special (p. 16)

Students prepare to write a biographical essay by setting up questions for an interview. To avoid embarrassment, you may want to ask students not to interview classmates or teachers for this assignment.

If equipment is available, students could tape their interviews.

Vocabulary words: biography, interview

Titles: An Invitation to Read (p. 17)

Students may have difficulty writing titles for their stories and poems. This activity helps students realize that titles are important. Titles are invitations to the reader.

Discussion questions: Why do stories have titles? What do titles tell us about books? How are titles like a welcome mat? How are titles similar to headlines? How are they different?

Remind students that a story or poem isn't finished unless it has a title.

Jeb Hopped, Skipped and Jumped (p. 18)

This activity can be tied into a review of verb tenses and agreement of verbs with nouns. List the letters from A to Z on the board. As a class, ask students to suggest action verbs that begin with each letter of the alphabet.

Student Writes Award-Winning Headlines (p. 19) and Astronauts Discover Life on Mars (p. 20)

Review action verbs with your class. Provide newspapers and magazines for students to use for these activities. The two questions on the first activity would be good ones for a class discussion. How are headlines like titles? How are headlines and titles different?

As a class, suggest headlines to describe events in your classroom. After students finish these two activities, ask them to go back and look at the headlines they wrote. Are there any unnecessary words that could be eliminated? Did they use action verbs? Give them time to look over their work and make changes.

Wee Willie Winkie (in the poetry section, page 109) provides additional practice in alliteration.

Vocabulary word: alliteration

Answer the Six Questions (p. 21)

The lead sentences of a good newspaper article answer the six questions: who, what, when, where, why and how.

Bring newspapers to class. Have students read the first two sentences of several articles, looking for the answers to all six questions.

Students can practice writing leads for other articles about events that occur at school, at home or in their community. Encourage them to complete the rest of the article. Compile the articles for a class newspaper. Take photos to go with the articles.

Tools of the Trade (p. 22)

Writers use many tools besides paper and pencils, typewriters and computers. Students learn the difference between a dictionary and thesaurus in **Tools of the Trade**. A thesaurus can be a valuable tool for young writers as long as they realize that words in a thesaurus are not necessarily synonyms. Caution them never to substitute a word from a thesaurus unless they are certain they know the meaning of the word.

Vocabulary words: dictionary, thesaurus

In Other Words (p. 23) and Up, Down, Over, Under (p. 24)

A synonym is a word with the same or similar meaning as another word. Authors often use synonyms to make their writing more interesting. Students receive additional practice in using a thesaurus and writing synonyms in these activities.

Discussion questions: How does the use of synonyms make writing more interesting? Why is it useful to know the antonym for a word?

Vocabulary words: thesaurus, synonym, substitute, antonym

Look It Up (p. 25)

Look It Up introduces students to other types of reference books that are helpful when writing. Encyclopedias, atlases, almanacs, newspapers, magazines and textbooks are types of reference books students need to become familiar with. Books about nature, countries, holidays, music, history, science or geology can provide answers to many questions. Students can't be expected to find answers if they don't know where to look.

Give students time in the reference section with the librarian. Ask the librarian to show students what types of reference books are available, where to find them and what types of information they contain.

Tie this activity in with a research project in another subject. Students could use reference books to find the answers to several questions on this worksheet.

Vocabulary words: atlas, almanac, reference, resources

Great Idea! (p. 26) and Don't Let Good Ideas Get Away (p. 27)

Starting an "idea file" encourages students to think ahead and prepare for future writing projects. Start a classroom Idea File. Write suggestions for topics and "what if" questions on index cards. Clip interesting pictures from magazines or headlines from newspapers. Encourage students to add suggestions to the idea file. When students are at a loss for something to write about, let them look through the class idea file.

Photocopy and enlarge the outline of the light bulb or draw one on a large piece of poster board. Post it in your classroom. Tie a pencil to a string attached to the poster. Invite students to add ideas to the poster for everyone to share. If good ideas come up in a class discussion on another subject, one of the students could add it to the light bulb.

At the end of this section you will find a list of topics to draw on when someone says, "I don't know what to write about."

What If? (p. 28)

Asking "what if" questions opens the door to unlimited possibilities for story ideas. Students may enjoy working on this activity in small groups. They could brainstorm to come up with a list of "what if" questions.

Why Write Letters? (p. 29), Writing a Friendly Letter (p. 30) and Writing a Business Letter (p. 31)

With the ease of long distance calling, letter writing is becoming a lost art, yet it is a form of writing that is still needed. Writing memos and letters is a critical part of many jobs.

Besides, it's fun to receive letters and the only way to get them is to write them. In these activities, students practice writing an informal friendly letter and a formal business letter.

Students who are interested in writing to a foreign pen pal can contact the **International Friendship League**, 55 Mount Vernon Street, Boston, MA 02108 or **World Pen Pals**, 1694 Como Avenue, St. Paul, MN 55108.

Invite students who receive replies to share their letters with the class.

Speak Up (p. 32) and Sound Off (p. 33)

The difference between facts and opinions is briefly introduced in **Speak Up**. The first section of the worksheet could be done as a class. Most students will not have any difficulty with the first five statements but may not think "Apple pie tastes better than spinach," is an opinion. Even though most people agree, this is an opinion, not a fact.

Make other statements. Let the class decide if they are facts or opinions.

Cut short editorials from your local newspaper for students to read. Students could work in groups to brainstorm ideas of editorial topics for kids.

Possible topics for editorials are listed in **Sound Off**. Students who feel strongly about another subject could write about that topic instead.

If appropriate, you could send student editorials to the local paper.

Vocabulary word: editorial

Stop, Look, Listen (p. 34); Picture This (p. 35); Welcome to Duncan's Cave (p. 36) and Get into the Scene (p. 37)

Students use observational skills to complete these four activities by writing stories based on illustrations.

Often, people look but do not see what is around them. Encourage students to become more observant. Give students five minutes and ask them to make a list of everything they see. When they finish, make a group list on the board by combining everyone's list. How many items were in the longest list? How many items are in the group list? What other items could be added to the group list?

Photographs and pictures from magazines can also be used for additional practice in observation and story starters. Students can use visual clues from the pictures to write stories.

Sharon's Magic Hat (p. 38), And Then What Happened? (p. 39) and What's Behind the Door? (p. 40)

Using visual clues, students combine drawing with predicting in these three activities.

Hold a story contest for one of these activities. Include as many categories as you can—funniest, scariest, most unusual, shortest, most imaginative, best character, best use of adjectives, neatest handwriting, best drawing, etc. Award several "honorable mentions" in each category.

Make a large title, "What's Behind the Door?" and hang it on your classroom door. Display student stories on the wall behind the door.

Vocabulary word: predict

What Am I? (p. 41) and Tell Me About It (p. 42)

Writing in the form of riddles introduces students to writing short descriptions. They practice writing longer descriptions in **Tell Me**

TLC10017 Copyright © Teaching & Learning Company, Carthage, IL 62321

About It by pretending to describe an object to someone from another planet.

Let students read their descriptions to the class. As they read, pretend you are the alien and don't know what the object looks like. Draw the object on the board as they read, using only their description. Does it look the way it should? If not, ask the student what he or she forgot to describe about the object.

Feel It (p. 43) and **Two Scents Worth** (p. 44)

Students explore the senses of touch and smell in these two activities.

Gather several objects with different textures. Put them in a small bag, one at a time. Have students reach in and touch the object without seeing it. Ask them to describe how it feels and guess what it is.

Gather several different scents in dark brown medicine bottles. You could use a few drops of lemon juice, peppermint oil, ammonia, some garlic, onion, rose petals, chocolate syrup, etc. Ask students to describe what they smell and guess what it is without looking at it.

Give Me an Example, Please (p. 45)

In this activity students define the meaning of words and explain words by providing examples of something similar.

Extend this activity by asking students to give examples of other words: *bread, soda, cartoon character, darkness, crackers, shovel, lamp, pen, carpet, bunk bed, sandwich, bathtub,* etc.

How Are They Alike? (p. 47), **I Am a . . .** (p. 48), **How Are They Different?** (p. 49) and **A Lot Like Me** (p. 50)

To compare objects means to look for ways they are alike. Some objects are easy to compare because they are quite similar. A car and a pickup truck have much in common. Some objects are more difficult to compare because they have very little in common, like a cloud and shaving cream.

To contrast objects means to look for ways they are different. Students are frequently asked to compare and contrast objects, ideas, books, poems and characters. These activities specify the difference between compare and contrast and give students practice in both.

In **How Are They Alike?** all the objects in the first group are alive, so students have at least one item in common to start. In the second group, all the items are inanimate, if students realize that a mouse can be part of a computer.

These worksheets would work well with small groups of students.

Students can use comparing and contrasting skills in science, social studies, geography, history and other subjects.

Happiness Is . . . (p. 91), **The Sunshine of My Life** (p. 123) and **A Beard Like a Bird's Nest** (p. 92) are other activities writing metaphors and similes. Encourage students to use metaphors and similes when completing **I Am a . . .**. For further practice comparing themselves to fictional characters, ask students to compare how a particular character solves a problem to how they would have solved the problem.

Im-Possibles (p.51)

Thinking of impossible situations can be another source of story ideas for students. They can select from a list of "Couldn't be's" or from their own ideas. The first part of this activity would work well as a class activity. Students can brainstorm to think of impossible situations that might make a good basis for a story.

A Different Way to Look at the World (p. 52); **As Tall as a Tree, as Small as a Bee** (p. 53) and **Three Wishes** (p. 54)

In an earlier activity, students are encouraged to ask "what if" questions. These three activities are also based on "what if" questions. Students could work together in small groups to brainstorm ideas for the prewriting portion of **As Tall as a Tree, as Small as a Bee**.

Students may enjoy reading *The Borrowers* by Mary Norton. The movie *Honey, I Shrunk the Kids* is another fun example of what it would be like to be much, much smaller.

Many fairy tales include characters who are granted three wishes, but rarely do they end up happily ever after. Usually, something about the wishes backfires and the characters end up worse off than they were in the beginning. **The Three Wishes** and **The Fisherman and His Wife** are fairy tales with this theme. The *Monkey's Paw* by W.W. Jacobs is also a good example of a wish that doesn't turn out the way the characters expect. Recommend this story to older students because it's rather scary.

Beyond Space and Time (p. 55)

Students plan a science fiction or fantasy story in this activity. They may enjoy reading stories and books by Isaac Asimov, Anne McCaffrey, Ray Bradbury, Robert Heinlin, J.R.R. Tolkien and Arthur C. Clark.

Redesign a Car (p. 56) and **A Game for Two** (p. 57)

Students use critical thinking skills as they **Redesign a Car** in pictures and words. Display the new models on the bulletin board. Discuss more innovative ideas in class.

Suggest other items students could redesign and improve: a mousetrap, a different topping for pizza, a new flavor of ice cream, a hat, car keys that don't sink to the bottom of a purse, dry water . . .

In **A Game for Two** students invent a new game using a limited number of items. Students can share their new games with their classmates.

One by One (p. 58) and **What Was the Question?** (p. 61)

Students look at illustrations, then draw and write a sequential story for **One by One**.

What Was the Question? provides additional practice in sequential and logical thinking. Have several students read their questions to the same answer. How many different questions did students think of for the same answer?

Put the Thingamabob on the Whatchacallit (p. 62) and Which Way? (p. 63)

Have you ever assembled a product using directions that were so confusing they might as well have been written in hieroglyphics?

Students receive additional practice in sequential thinking as they write step-by-step directions for completing a simple task. Before students begin **Put the Thingamabob on the Whatchacallit**, write directions as a class to complete a simple task like planting a seed, sending a birthday card, making a paper airplane or drawing a 45° angle. Write the steps on the board as students suggest what to do. Include every detail, no matter how minor and every step in order, no matter how obvious. Leave room between steps so you can go back and add a missed step if needed.

To complete this activity, students could work in pairs as they practice writing clear directions to complete one of the tasks listed. Ask students to read their directions out loud. Work together as a class to improve the directions.

Students write clear directions and draw a map to explain how to get from one place to another in **Which Way?**

Could You Be More Specific? (p. 64) and Exactly What Do You Mean? (p. 65)

Students move from general to specific words and terms as a warm-up for future writing activities. Write several short, general sentences on the board. As a class, work on rewriting the sentences to make them more specific.

Vocabulary word: specific

Help Wanted (p. 66)

As young writers develop, they often tend to use too many words. This activity helps them condense material and write concisely.

Bring in the classified section from a

Sunday newspaper. Write several ads on the board. Have students suggest words that could be eliminated or more concise ways to write the ad.

Here is one possible way of rewriting the first ad: For Sale: 1937 pink Dodge. Completely restored. Call 555-1212 after 6 p.m.

Discussion topic: What other types of writing need to be clear and concise?

Leave a Message (p. 67)

Students are asked to use critical thinking skills to find a way to leave a message without paper or pencil. The items they have to work with are an open can of chocolate syrup, two feathers, a bag of mini marshmallows and a piece of rope.

What's Your Advice? (p. 68)

Read several of the replies to the class to initiate a class discussion. Since students may feel self-conscious about what they wrote, it's not necessary to name the authors of the replies.

Check Your Work (p. 69) and A Penny Saved . . . (p. 70)

Prewriting, rewriting and polishing are steps in the writing process. Remind students to take one more step before handing in their final draft. They should proofread their work.

Students practice proofreading a short story which includes spelling, capitalization and punctuation errors, duplication of words and use of the incorrect form of words (*bee* instead of *be*, *they're* instead of *their . . .*).

How many students caught the extra *is* in the title of this activity?

Students can work together to proofread each other's writing.

Answer key. Errors can be found in bold type.

> Mr. Nobody and Miss Somebody plan to **to** get married soon. One **smalll** problem is **is** stopping **thrm** from setting the date.
>
> Miss Somebody wants **too**

keep her last **Name** after they get married. **mr.** Nobody wants her to change it. He thinks she **sould** be Mrs (period missing) Nobody. He wants **they're** children to be little Nobodys.

Miss Somebody likes her **her** last name. She wants to **to** be a Somebody **(period missing)** If they have children, **th** girls could be Somebodys and the boys could **bee** Nobodys. Mr. Nobody doesn't **not** agree.

Miss **somebody** thought they **culd** use both names and be Mr. and Mrs. Somebody-Nobody. **that ideas** didn't make Mr. Nobody happy either.

If they don't find an answer to **the** their problem, there won't be a wedding **(period missing)** Maybe they should both change their last names to **jones**.

Know Your Characters (p. 71) and Bring Characters to Life (p. 73)

Before students begin these two activities, ask them to name characters they've read about. Have them give reasons why the characters are memorable. Discuss a specific character from a book or story the class has read. How many specific details can they recall about the main character?

In these two activities, students get to know potential characters by making up background information about them. When they finish, they're asked to write a short story using what they've learned about the characters.

Vocabulary word: character

Clash of the Characters (p. 74)

Students learn that conflict makes stories more interesting. They are asked to think of a story idea that involves conflict and find several solutions to resolve the conflict.

It Depends on How You Look at It (p. 75)

How often do eyewitnesses to the same event relate different, even contradictory details about what they've seen? Is it because they're unreliable? Because they're not telling the truth?

Often it has to do with their "closeness" to an event or how personally involved they are. A woman who saw her child fall from a tree would probably "see" the event differently if the child were a stranger.

Ask students to think about an upcoming vacation from the teacher's point of view and from their parents' point of view. Suggest other situations students can look at from other points of view.

What Would They Say? (p. 76) and Show Time (p. 77)

Writing dialogue that sounds natural can be difficult even for experienced writers. Most young writers experience difficulty writing natural sounding dialogue. Encourage students to speak dialogue before they write it. Have them listen to the words. Do the words seem stilted? How can they make dialogue sound more natural?

Review the proper use of quotation marks in dialogue. Record a conversation between you and the class during a discussion period. As the students listen to the recording, they'll notice that people don't always speak in complete sentences. What else do they notice about dialogue?

Combine **Show Time** with a puppet-making art activity.

Vocabulary word: dialogue

"Come into My Parlor . . ." (p. 78) and The Little Dog Laughed (p. 79)

Children are surrounded by personified characters from little on. Books and stories use animals and objects that talk. They watch animated characters in cartoons and television commercials.

"Come into My Parlor . . ."

combines dialogue and personification. Students stretch their imaginations as they make up a conversation between two objects or animals. Read two or three Aesop's fables to

the class as examples of personification before students begin **The Little Dog Laughed**.

Vocabulary word: personification

Don't Count Your Chickens . . . (p. 80)

A parable is a story with a moral or one that teaches a lesson. The moral may be stated at the end of the story or merely implied. Read several Aesop's fables to the class. Other good examples of parables are "The Emperor's New Clothes" and "The Ugly Duckling" by Hans Christian Andersen.

Vocabulary words: parable, moral

Why Do Zebras Have Stripes? (p. 81) and Why Does the Sun Rise in the East? (p. 82)

Without scientific explanations, people had no way to explain the world around them. Myths are stories from ancient cultures that explain natural phenomena or the origins of a people (creation myths). Supernatural beings frequently appear in myths as gods and goddesses with extraordinary powers or talents.

Writing modern myths lets students stretch their imaginations. Before students begin writing their answers in the activity **Why Do Zebras Have Stripes?** they could work together in small groups to think of answers for one of the questions. Ask each group to share their best answer with the class.

Read several myths from various cultures to your class before they begin the activity **Why Does the Sun Rise in the East?** Collect the myths your students write, type them and make a class anthology. Ask students to illustrate their myths.

What Does It Mean? (p. 83)

Proverbs are familiar sayings that express some type of folk wisdom. Students are encouraged to look for the meaning of several proverbs, then write one of their own. Younger children may need to complete this activity as a group.

Grizzly Bear Day (p. 84)

Students write a legend of their own similar to the one about the

Groundhog who sees his shadow on February 2. You could plan this as a Groundhog Day activity and tie it in with a science unit on groundhogs (woodchucks) or hibernation.

Call Me Ishmael (p. 85) and From Third to First (p. 86)

After reading first person examples, students are asked to write sentences in first person. In **From Third to First** they rewrite a short paragraph written in third person.

Ask students to list reasons why they like reading first person stories and third person stories. Which do they prefer? Why?

Only a Dream? (p. 87)

Use this activity as an opportunity to review the difference between common nouns and proper nouns. Review capitalization of proper nouns and correct usage of pronouns.

From A to Z (p. 88) and A Dark, Stormy Night (p. 89)

For additional practice recognizing adjectives, assign a page of text in a story for students to read. Ask them to list all the adjectives they find on the page.

Combine all the adjectives students list on this activity (**From A to Z**) on a master class adjective list. Post the list for students to use when writing.

Discussion questions: How do adjectives make writing more interesting? Is it possible to use too many adjectives?

Vocabulary word: adjective

How Now? (p. 90)

Adverbs modify verbs, adjectives and other adverbs. They describe how or when something occurs. Use this worksheet as the beginning of further study of adverbs. Again, students can use the A to Z method to make a list of adverbs.

Discussion question: How do adverbs make writing more interesting?

Vocabulary word: adverb

Happiness Is a Perfect Checkup . . . (p. 91)

A metaphor is a figure of speech that compares two unlike objects or ideas without using the words *like* or *as*. To Linus, security is a warm snugly blanket. To Charlie Brown, happiness might be getting to kick the football before Lucy yanks it away. Students could brainstorm to think of other examples of metaphors for characters from cartoons, comics and stories.

Write the best examples from the worksheet Happiness Is . . . on colored cards and display them around your classroom. Another activity on writing metaphors can be found in the poetry section of this book.

Discussion question: How do metaphors make writing more interesting?

Vocabulary word: metaphor

A Beard Like a Bird's Nest (p. 92)

A simile is a figure of speech that compares two different objects or ideas by using the words *like* or *as*. Ask students to select their best similes and read them to the class.

Discussion question: How do similes make stories more interesting?

Vocabulary word: simile

Treasure Hunt (p. 93), Sea Hunt (p. 94) and Paint a Word Picture (p. 95)

Students use their imagination to describe an undersea adventure and what they might find in a treasure chest.

Artists can paint and draw beautiful pictures with paint. Authors can use words to paint word pictures as vivid as any found on canvas.

Buy Me (p. 96), Why Buy Spinach Ice Cream (p. 97), Buckle Up (p. 98) and Vote for Vince (p. 99)

We are surrounded by thousands of ads every day in newspapers and magazines, on billboards, radio and TV. Each ad is designed to catch our attention, to convince us to buy a specific product, vote for a certain candidate or use the services of a restaurant, hotel or other business. Public service ads remind us of safety rules: buckle up, don't pollute, etc.

Before students begin these activities, cut ads from newspapers and magazines. Evaluate the ads as a class. Discuss ways used to appeal to buyers.

These activities encourage students to evaluate ads and allow them to write an ad for a product, a person and an idea.

Provide newspapers and magazines for students to use in the first activity, **Buy Me**. Invite students to think of other ideas to sell in **Buckle Up**.

Discussion questions: Why are celebrities and cartoon characters used to promote products? Do ads have anything to do with the quality of the product, service or person being promoted? Can ads be misleading?

Words That Aren't but Should Be (p. 100)

Students can have fun making up words as outrageous as anything Dr. Seuss ever invented in **Words That Aren't but Should Be**.

Read *The Lorax* or another favorite Seuss book to your class. Ask students to stop you when come to a made-up word. Write the word on the board. When you finish the story, ask students to define the words you wrote.

Ask students to name the best made-up word they wrote. The rest of the class can try to guess what it means.

A Million Times (p. 101) and Super Snail to the Rescue (p. 102)

These two worksheets encourage students to use hyperboles and create their own superheroes. Have the class discuss superheroes they've read about or seen in cartoons and movies. What do the superheroes have in common? How are they different?

The title **Super Snail to the Rescue** is ironical. Discuss irony with your class and how it is used in literature.

TEACHER NOTES: WRITING POETRY

Rhyme Time (p. 103)

Students are familiar with nursery rhymes and other types of poetry that rhyme. In fact, many students will include rhyme as part of the definition of a poem. The first part of this poetry section is devoted to poems that rhyme and/or ones that have a specific format.

Rhyme Time is a warm-up exercise to get students started writing rhyming poetry.

One, Two, Buckle My Shoe (p. 104)

Couplets are easy and fun to write. Students are asked to write the second line to complete the couplets in this activity.

Read the nursery rhyme "One, Two, Buckle My Shoe" as an example of a poem written in couplets. As a class, have students suggest new lines for the poem, counting by fives or tens.

As an added challenge, students could write a second couplet to go with one on the worksheet to produce a four-line rhyming poem.

Encourage students to read their favorite couplets to the class.

The Tennessee Fair (p. 105) and The Old Man with a Beard (p. 106)

Limericks are fun to read and write. Read the poem "Hickory, Dickory, Dock." How many students recognize this as a limerick? Point out how the last words of lines 1, 2 and 5 rhyme.

The Tennessee Fair is a limerick writing activity based on the song/poem "The Animal Fair" which is also a limerick.

Singing or humming this song will give students a feel for the rhythm of the words.

In the style of master limerick writer, Edward Lear, students write another limerick in **The Old Man with a Beard**. Challenge students to come up with other limericks on different subjects.

Class discussion topic: Why are limericks "fun" types of poems?

Vocabulary word: limerick

Sing a Silly Song (p. 107)

Songs are essentially poetry set to music. Some rhyme; some don't. By rewriting the words to well-known, simple songs, students warm up for writing other original poems in later activities.

Invite several students to sing the new words to a song as a four-part round.

What's That Noise? (p. 108)

A word or group of words that imitates a sound is called onomatopoeia. Read Edgar Allen Poe's "The Bells" to the class. The first time you read it, ask students to close their eyes and listen to the sound of the words. Read it a second time. Ask students to raise their hands when they hear onomatopoeia.

Students can look for examples of onomatopoeia in other prose and poetry.

Ask each student to read one of his onomatopoeic words. Have the other members of the class try to determine what the sound describes.

Vocabulary word: onomatopoeia

Wee Willie Winkie (p. 109)

Alliteration is the use of several words beginning with the same letter or sound. Sometimes alliteration is used in prose, but it is more common in poetry.

For a fun example of alliteration, read *The Berenstains' B Book* by Stanley and Janice Berenstain (Random House, 1971). Tongue twisters are good examples of alliteration. You'll find lots of examples in *My Tang's Tungled and Other Ridiculous Situations*.

Invite students to write their own tongue twisters on the board. Challenge the class to read them without getting their tongues tangled.

Vocabulary word: alliteration

A Sign of Spring (p. 110) and Dinosaurs (p. 111)

Haiku poetry originated in Japan about 600 years ago. Each poem consists of three unrhymed lines and a specific number of syllables in each line.

Review how to syllabify words before starting these activities. Write several three- and four-syllable words on the board (beautiful, everlasting, Saturday, interesting, January . . .) As a class, count the syllables in each word.

Read examples of haiku to your class. Write several on the board. Count the syllables in each line.

For additional practice writing haiku, suggest other topics like school, a holiday, a day of the week, a person, weather or transportation.

Vocabulary word: haiku

A Poem in Five Lines (p. 112) and Other Ways to Write Cinquains (p. 113)

A cinquain is a five-line, nonrhyming poem developed by Adelaide Crapsey in the late 1800s. Several acceptable forms of cinquains have evolved. Students practice writing two types of cinquains in these activities.

Vocabulary word: cinquain

A Story Poem (p. 114)

Read several narrative poems to your class. Examples are "Old Mother Hubbard," "Casey at the Bat" by Ernest Lawrence Thayer, "The Pied Piper of Hamlin" by Robert Browning, "Lincoln" by Nancy Byrd Turner, "Paul Revere's Ride" and "Hiawatha's Childhood" by Henry Wadsworth Longfellow and "A Visit from St. Nicholas" by Clement Clarke Moore.

Vocabulary word: lyric

A Poem from a Word (p. 115)

Acrostic poems begin with a word written vertically on the page. The first word of each line begins with the letter on that line. The subject of the poem is always the word used to begin the poem. The lines do not have to rhyme. Students can use any number of words or syllables in each line.

If students have trouble thinking of a starting word for an acrostic poem, offer them one of these ideas: trees, Monday, ideas, friends, school, fish, lemon or kite.

After students have completed this activity, suggest that they write an acrostic poem about themselves using their first or last name as the beginning word. Students with long names (Cynthia, Alexander, etc.) may prefer to use a shorter nickname for their poem.

Vocabulary word: acrostic

Visual Poems (p. 116)

In the 1970s, many poets moved away from traditional poetry and began experimenting with unusual forms of poetry. Some began writing what were called "concrete poems"—ones written in the shape of the subject of the poem.

This type of poetry is very fluid and offers unlimited possibilities, even for students who have difficulty writing poetry. Concrete poems may be compact or spread across an entire sheet of paper. This activity would work well in an art class. Encourage students to use colored pencils, markers, crayons or other media to write their poems.

These poems make a great bulletin board display because they're so visually appealing.

Doodle a Poem (p. 117)

Students can relax and doodle a while to begin this activity. Doodle poems are fun to write because there isn't any right or wrong way to do it. This activity can be used as a warm-up exercise for writing other types of free verse.

Wander a While (p. 118)

Free association is a technique similar to brainstorming but much less rigid. Poets may use free association as a warm-up exercise before starting a poem.

Do free association with your class. Start with any word (purple, vanilla, Hawaii, pincushion, computer, rutabaga . . .).

Ask one student to say the first word he thinks of. Ask another student to say the first word she thought of when she heard the last response. Don't stop for explanations. Continue with this until everyone in the class has had a turn. Where did you end up? Chances are the last word had absolutely nothing to do with the one you started with.

Discussion topic: How can free association help you write a poem?

A Hunting We Will Go (p. 119) and Trees (p. 120)

These two activities encourage students to write a free verse poem about an animal and a tree.

Students may enjoy reading or listening to *The Giving Tree* by Shel Silverstein.

The Sunshine of My Life (p. 123)

A metaphor is a figure of speech that compares two different objects or ideas without using the words *like* or *as*. Review the activity, "Happiness Is . . ." in the prose section of this book.

When students finish this activity, ask them to rewrite their favorite metaphor as a poem on a 3" x 5" index card. Display the cards on the bulletin board.

A Few of My Favorite Things (p. 124)

List poems are exactly what they sound like, a list of items related in some way.

Play a recording, sing or read the words to the song "My Favorite Things." Ask students how this song is like a list poem.

Students could write a list poem at Thanksgiving about things they are thankful for. Challenge students to write an alliterative list poem on items of a certain color.

Talk about the difference between things we "need" and things we "want." Students could write a list poem of things they need or want, but remind them to remember the difference.

A Gift That Keeps on Giving (p. 125)

Tie this activity in with an upcoming special occasion or holiday like Christmas, Hanukkah, Valentine's Day or Mother's Day. Provide fancy stationery or paper for students to write their final version of their gift poem. Students could roll up their poems and tie them with fancy ribbon.

TLC10017 Copyright © Teaching & Learning Company, Carthage, IL 62321

200 CREATIVE WRITING IDEAS

1	a discovery you made	50	follow a rainbow
2	a door with no doorknob	51	football players
3	a locked door	52	forgetting a birthday
4	air traffic controller	53	forgetting your homework
5	alien voices on the radio	54	fresh cinnamon rolls
6	aliens from Mercury	55	Friday
7	April	56	fried tennis shoes
8	August	57	friends
9	bee stings	58	frogs
10	being a chess piece	59	frustrations
11	being in a parade	60	full moon
12	being in a wheelchair	61	funniest thing you ever saw
13	best day of your life	62	games: invent new ones
14	best idea you ever had	63	getting a wish
15	black jelly beans	64	getting a new pet
16	blowing up 100 balloons	65	getting elected
17	blue baboons	66	giant sunflowers
18	books you've read	67	going away to school
19	bothersome brothers	68	good jokes
20	building a tree house	69	great gifts to give
21	changing places with someone for a day	70	green hair
22	circus clowns	71	gremlins in your desk
23	collecting seashells	72	Halloween
24	conversations with yourself	73	hang gliding
25	create a cartoon character	74	having an arm in a cast
26	crocodiles that smile	75	helpful elves
27	dancing	76	hiding from a dinosaur
28	darkness	77	hobbies
29	daylight savings time	78	horses that talk
30	days hot enough to . . .	79	ice cream melting
31	December	80	invent something
32	difficult questions	81	January
33	dolls that talk	82	jobs you'd like to have
34	dreams	83	joyous occasions
35	eagles	84	July
36	early morning	85	June
37	eating fresh applesauce	86	kings
38	embarrassing moments	87	kite flying
39	exploring a cave	88	life in the desert
40	exploring the North Pole	89	life is a plate of liver
41	favorite color	90	lightning
42	favorite food	91	lions
43	favorite holiday	92	living in an igloo
44	favorite song, book or movie	93	loneliness
45	February	94	losing something important
46	finding a diamond mine	95	losing your house key
47	finding a treasure map	96	loss of a pet
48	finding gold	97	magicians
49	first day of school	98	March
		99	Mars

100	May	151	Sunday
101	meeting a celebrity	152	sunsets
102	meeting a giant	153	surfing in the ocean
103	meeting a leprechaun	154	swimming in the ocean
104	meeting the President	155	taking a test
105	memories	156	talking goldfish
106	missing a friend	157	talking to your computer
107	Monday	158	tangled yo-yo strings
108	money	159	taste of lemons
109	most embarrassing moment	160	the Queen of England
110	most unusual present ever received	161	thick ketchup
111	mountain climbing	162	things you'd like to change
112	movies you've seen	163	thunderstorms
113	neighbors	164	Thursday
114	nighttime fears	165	time travel
115	November	166	traveling to Zanzibar
116	October	167	trip to Jupiter
117	opening a mysterious box	168	trip to the zoo
118	parachute jumping	169	truck drivers
119	peaches without pits	170	Tuesday
120	penguins as pets	171	tulip trees
121	perfect presents	172	turtles talking
122	picnics at the beach	173	unexpected surprise
123	plaid zebras	174	unknown paths
124	purple room	175	unusual rain
125	reindeer	176	upside-down umbrellas
126	relatives	177	vacations you'd like to take
127	rhinoceros named Ralph	178	view from a hot air balloon
128	rutabaga soup	179	view from the Empire State Building
129	riding in an airplane	180	violins
130	riding in a submarine	181	visiting Venus
131	Saturday	182	visiting your grandparents
132	scary things	183	walk through a rain forest
133	seeing an antelope	184	wearing glasses
134	September	185	weather
135	seven seasick sailors	186	Wednesday
136	shadows	187	whale watching
137	shivering	188	what if you were an onion
138	short giraffe	189	what owls do at night
139	sitting on a cloud	190	what you saw through the window
140	skinny elephants		
141	sledding	191	what's in a kangaroo's pocket
142	sneezes	192	who lives in the hole in the ground
143	snuggling under a warm quilt	193	why I like . . .
144	someone you'd like to meet	194	window to another dimension
145	something you are proud of	195	windy days
146	spiders in your room	196	winter sports
147	staying in the hospital	197	worst photograph
148	striking oil in your backyard	198	X rays of someone's brain
149	striped paint	199	yellow rain slickers
150	stuck zippers	200	you